MW01231805

By the Grace of God...

I AM

A JOURNEY INTO THE DISCOVERY OF MY TRUE IDENTITY

MAURICE E. ROGERS

Please Rate and Review

If you enjoy the book 'By the Grace of God... I Am', please leave a positive review and a favourable star rating on its online store page! Thank you, I really appreciate it.

You can go directly to the review page by using your mobile device to scan this QR code:

Or by this link: ***https://newkosmos.us/review***

By the Grace of God... I Am

A Journey into the Discovery of My True Identity

Maurice E. Rogers

MAURICE E. ROGERS

2020

Copyright © 2020 by Maurice E. Rogers

All rights reserved. This book or any portion thereof may not be reproduced or used in any manner whatsoever without the express written permission of the publisher except for the use of brief quotations in a book review or scholarly journal.

First Printing: 2020

ISBN 9798561239762

Maurice E. Rogers

Apt#3 Leroy Nichols Building

Kingstown Park, Kingstown, VC0120

Saint Vincent and the Grenadines

www.newkosmos.us

I hope this book is a blessing to you!

If you are looking for a resource on how to live in your new identity, consider subscribing to
The New Kosmos Masterclass

This online seminar is a tremendous resource which:

- Presents with your Identity in Christ
- Positions you in the Kingdom of God, and
- Prepares you to Live Abundantly.

Receive clarity on what is available to you as a Kingdom Citizen, and a more detailed picture of your potential as a Child of God.

The New Kosmos Masterclass

Many have come to discover their true identity through the 'Living in the New Kosmos' Masterclass.

Obtain the clearest understanding of your Identity in Christ.

Live successfully and victoriously a life of Peace, Purpose and Prosperity.

Sign Up Now!

Scan the QR Code or go to *newkosmos.us/masterclass*

Dedication

This book is dedicated to my two daughters:

Sadé

and

Zayithe.

Contents

Acknowledgements

Apart from my Heavenly Father, who of course is the one that orders all things for my good, I would like to thank those select few persons who have personally helped and influenced me in my spiritual growth.

These persons know who they are, but two are worthy of special mention.

- Gregory Rogers.

- Gideon Soleyn.

These persons have always been there for me along my spiritual walk.

Thank you.

Preface

Hello to you. I want to congratulate you for making the bold decision to purchase my book. I am very confident that it was the Lord who influenced that decision, for in this book lies the insight that many have been deprived of.

This book will change your life in a positive way, even if only a little, but I do hope that it will be much.

Let me tell you a little about myself. Around the year 2017, I experienced a spiritual renewal that turned my whole paradigm upside down and inside out. The result of this was that I was impressed to thoroughly go through all of my denominational beliefs, to see if they comprehensively fit in with a holistic narrative of the scripture. Unfortunately, I discovered that they only had a limited agreement with the narrative of the scriptures. One of the biggest flaws of the denominational narrative was that it relied heavily on the King James Version translation. Having gotten access to interlinear and literal translations of the scripture, I could see that many conclusions were made based on assumptions, misunderstanding and errors in the translation.

In addition to this, I began to see more clearly what Christ's mission was all about. Over the next three years I presented my discoveries to a small fellowship group that I had become a part of. The more I presented, the more I learned. The more I learned, the more I became convinced that I should write these things in a book.

I believe that the information in this book is essential to everyone. It is my firm belief that without this knowledge, it is impossible to have a fulfilling spiritual life. Many people are terrified of the God they worship and have an absolutely devastating view of God's opinion of them. The information in this book has helped me come to a spiritual place where I am confident of my heavenly Father's unconditional love and acceptance of me.

Often whenever I meet a friend, and I try to tell them my understanding, every word out of my mouth is met with a question and an objection. It is like playing verbal ping pong. Added to that, the typical five or ten minute meeting is way too insufficient to communicate my understanding effectively. Inadequate information usually results in us parting ways with my friend thinking, "Maurice has lost his mind!"

I reasoned that if I can put a book in the hand of a friend, and they could read it in their own time, at their own pace, then it would be a much better way to communicate my understanding.

I have strived to make this book a fair balance of simplicity, yet with enough detail that both a bible novice and theologian would have enough information to understand what I believe.

This book however, is by no means complete in terms of all the information on this topic. I have much more evidence. By the time this book is published, I may have even more. But I am satisfied that it is enough, and it is more than I had, when I began my investigation into the matter.

May the Lord give you the rest that I received through this knowledge. If this book has blessed you, please leave a positive review on its online store page wherever you have purchased it. Also recommend this book to your friends and family. I believe that it would make a great gift also.

Introduction

This book seeks to transition the reader from the earth to heaven, from the flesh to the spirit, from the natural to the spiritual. Its sole objective is to help the reader to see clearly the issues that plague humanity's ability to have a satisfying relationship with the Creator. The author, through his own spiritual journey, leads the reader through the seeming forest of the scripture, cutting a clear path to the true identity obtained by God for humanity.

The ideas and concepts in this book are not associated with, nor garnered from, any denomination or religion as far as the author is aware. Every view in this book is based solely on the scripture and the author's application of the scripture in his contemporary context and understanding.

Some of the concepts this book sheds light on are:

- What is the significance of the Tree of the Knowledge of Good and Evil, and the Tree of Life, in our lives today.

- What is the Image and Likeness of God.

- What is God's True opinion of you.

- What does it mean to be 'in Christ.'

- What is the new creation.

- How to be born of the spirit.

- How to 'put on Christ.'

- How to 'pray in the spirit.'

The author of this book sought to take its concepts from the scriptures in a very honest way, without skewing or over-explaining the plainness of the words. As such, the understanding and application of some scriptures may seem unconventional compared to traditional interpretations.

The various Bible translations employed for the many scripture quotations throughout this book have purposely not been given. The author wanted to take away from the reader any opportunity of prejudice. Many persons automatically disregard a truth based on which Bible version it is taken from.

It is recommended that this book be read in its correct sequence of chapter by chapter, for each chapter builds upon the previous.

Enjoy and be blessed!

CHAPTER 1
Who am I? Who are you?

Who am I? Who are you? Maybe you have never really given it much thought. I can't say that I've ever really given this profound question much, if any thought, until recent times. When I really did think about it, I realized that who I assumed I was, had been based on what was told to me by other people. In other words, my presumed identity was the sum total of other people's opinions about me. As an infant, I came into this world and all I knew was that I am. I knew that I existed, I was aware of myself, my feelings, my thoughts, my desires, my fears, my curiosities. But it was those persons around me who told me who they thought I was. *"You are a Baby! A bad boy, a good boy. You are Maurice, you are Junior, you are a Rogers. You are cute, you are naughty, the favorite."*

As I grew into a child, there were more voices telling me who I am. *"You are a child, a student, the kid with the glasses, the best friend, the sworn enemy. You are the brightest, the smartest, the dumbest, the silliest. Creative, yet unimaginative. You are handsome, ugly, intelligent, nerdy, brave, cowardly, extroverted, introverted."* These voices were conflicting in their opinion of me. Depending on the circumstances of my encounters with them, and the nature of my relationship to them, people would tell me who they thought I am. Then as a young man, I became identified by the jobs that I was employed to do. *"You are the pump attendant, the timekeeper, the graphic artist, the production manager."* I also had the honor of being called *"Daddy!"* as I stepped into the role of a father.

> »   *These voices were conflicting in their opinion of me. De-*
> *pending on the circumstances of my encounters with them,*
> *and the nature of my relationship to them, people would*
> *tell me who they thought I am.*

Just as I entered my 30's, I was given a new identity, as I was baptized into the Christian religion. As we should know, there are countless sects of Christianity, called denominations. The particular denomination into which I was accepted, told me that it was the *'True Church.'* I was told that by being part of that denomination, I was not just a Christian, but a special type of Christian, different from all the other Christians in all the other denominations. *"You are not just a Christian, you are a [name of denomination] Christian!"*

For the next 19 years, I invested a lot into that denominational identity. The denomination sought to identify me as an inextricable part of it. And so I believed that was who I am. It was as if I was the denomination. I was personally offended if I thought the denomination was being attacked in any way. Everything was done to not portray the denomination in *'a negative light.'* I was diligent in learning the denomination's teachings concerning God and Jesus, and also what they taught concerning who I am. I felt great pride and happiness in my denominational identity, and I embraced it wholeheartedly.

While being part of that denomination, I read the Bible ceaselessly. Granted, I read the Bible under the guidance of the denomination's opinion of its teachings, but at least I read it. In fact, several times I read through the Bible. I was good at presenting the denomination's view of the Bible. So my identity evolved. *"You are deacon, elder, preacher, evangelist, teacher, leader, coordinator."*

There I was having all of these opinions about who I am. But as

I came to discover, none of these opinions and identities were really the true *me*. At any point in time, those identities could change, and indeed many of them had changed and did change. I was no longer a child or a pump attendant. And depending on the circumstance, I could be introverted or extroverted. At the time, I was no longer serving as a deacon. So these identities were not *me*, they were assumed and artificial. They were not who *I am*.

It really was an eye-opener to me to discover that my occupations, my denominational membership and offices, and even my behaviors, were *not* who I am. I simply played the roles, I adapted my behavior to fit the situations, but that was not who I am. These roles were as garments, which I wore, some for longer periods than others. But a garment is not the person wearing it, nor is the person his or her garment, so too was I not these roles that I performed.

When I could see that clearly, the question remained, *who am I?* At some point in our lives, we all need to know who we really are. Unfortunately, there are so many voices telling us who we are, and most time those voices really seek to tell us *who they want us to be*. Is there really a way to know who you are?

I decided that I should enquire of the one person who seemed to know exactly who he really was. He was not an obscure nor an unknown recluse. In fact he is probably the most widely known man on earth. His name was Jesus of Nazareth.

CHAPTER 2
The Son of Our Humanity

I believe that we all need to know who we really are. It seems to me that many of us assume that the roles that life has given us – whether providentially, accidentally or naturally – are an indication of who we are. However, I have come to understand that we are not those roles. Neither are we who our parents, friends, enemies, society, religion or circumstances may have told us we are. We are immensely greater and of more importance than our circumstances dictate. Why do I say this? Because this is what I see when I look to the person whom billions agree was the greatest man to ever live – Jesus of Nazareth.

Consider that Jesus was not a wealthy person, as we esteem wealth. He did not come from an upper class, rich neighborhood. He did not live in a palace. In fact, his birth happened in a smelly stable and a feeding-trough was his cradle. His immediate sphere of influence was among a peculiar race of people with a peculiar religion. He even died at a young age.

Yet this man had an extraordinary understanding of who he was. His self-understanding propelled him to be the most influential person in all of earth's history. Jesus demonstrated his understanding of his true identity in a rather extreme way. He consistently referred to himself as the *'Son of Humanity'* – in the Third Person perspective, almost as if he was speaking of someone else. For example, instead of Jesus saying, *"I will go to Jerusalem,"* he would say, *"The Son of Humanity will go to Jerusalem."*

Here are some examples of Jesus referring to his *'Son of Humanity'* identity in the Third Person perspective.

- *"The foxes have burrows, and the birds of the heavens*

*have nests; but **the Son of Humanity** has nowhere to recline his head."* (Matt 8:20)

• *"**The Son of Humanity** is about to be betrayed into the hands of humanity."* (Matt 17:22)

• *"**The Son of Humanity** comes not to be ministered unto, but to minister..."* (Matt 20:28)

Notice in these and all other instances, Jesus never specifically said, *"**I am** the Son of Humanity."* He never claimed his *'Son of Humanity'* identity as who he really was! Thirty times in Matthew's gospel, Jesus always referred to this identity *in the Third Person view* as the *'Son of Humanity.'*

The Greek phrase *'huiou tou anthrōpou'* that many bible translations render as the *'Son of Man'*, is better rendered as *'Son of Humanity'* since the Greek word *'anthrōpou'* means *'mankind or humanity.'* While he never directly said he was the Son of Humanity, there however was *a definite emphasis by Jesus on that humanity.* This is also quite interesting, because in the scripture, the *'Son of Humanity'* is not exclusive to Jesus, but a Hebrew term that was used to refer to all humanity. In Psalm 8:4, the psalmist asked, *"**What is man**, that you are mindful of him? And **the son of humanity**, that you visit him?"* Notice the Hebrew parallel statements equate *'man'* [Hebrew *'enosh'*] with the *'son of humanity'* [Hebrew *'adam'*]. The Hebrew word *'adam'* shows that the *'son of humanity'* is literally the *'son of Adam'*, indicating that this term includes all of Adam's descendants. So, it seems to me that Jesus was purposefully emphasizing his *'Son of Humanity'* identity, to let us know that he was one of us. While at the same time, he also seemed to acknowledge his understanding that this identity *was not him.*

Jesus' apostles also attested that his humanity was just like that of his kindred. Paul wrote: *"Forasmuch then as the children are partakers of flesh and blood, **he also himself likewise partook of the same**... Wherefore **in all things it was essential for him to be made like unto his brethren**..."* (Heb 2:14,17). Evidently, Jesus was completely human, in all things, in every particular like his Jewish brethren. His body, mind, memory, intellect, emotions and physical strength were just like theirs, capable of doing what they could do, and as well, incapable of what they were incapable of. The systems of his body – the circulatory, digestive, excretory, endocrine, immune, reproductive and nervous systems functioned exactly like theirs.

I therefore believe that Jesus pointed to his *'Son of Humanity'* identity as a way of letting us know that he was the ideal human. He was the Son of *'Our Humanity.'* I have come to understand that whatever God was accomplishing through Jesus' humanity, he would likewise accomplish through our humanity! Jesus wanted us to have a new perspective on what humanity really should look like, what humanity was really capable of. The *'Son of Humanity'* was God's ideal for all of us. Until that point in time, humanity had never seen such an ideal in the flesh. Yes, many wise men may have spoken of lofty standards, and waxed eloquently about the perfect man. Yet Jesus was the first since Adam, to actually portray such a person. *I have come to see that remarkably, what God had accomplished with Jesus, He intended to accomplish for all Sons of Humanity, beginning with those first believers in Christ!*

» *I therefore believe that Jesus pointed to his 'Son of Humanity' identity as a way of letting us know that he was the ideal human. Jesus wanted us to have a new perspective on what humanity really should look like, what humanity was really capable of. The 'Son of Humanity' was God's ideal for all of us.*

6

As much as I could see that Jesus depicted the ideal Son of Humanity, just as human as me, yet I couldn't help but think that his self-awareness and self-perception, was quite unlike anyone else before him. Then it hit me. Just like I had been given those multiple identities, which I wore and played the roles, similarly the *'Son of Humanity'* was an identity that Jesus had been given! It was a role that he played, but it was not his true identity.

Listen to how the scripture sheds light on this. Speaking of Jesus' mission to this world, the prophet wrote: *"Therefore coming into the world, He says: 'Sacrifice and offering You have not desired, but **a body You have prepared for me**.'"* (Heb 10:5). Who is the *'me'* in this verse? It is someone for whom a body had been prepared. That indicates that they had existed apart from that body and before that body had been prepared. The human body was prepared for that person, the *'me.'* In the context of the verse, Jesus was the *'me'* that it was speaking of. But even more significantly, this verse tells us that the *'me'* or the *'I'* aspect of a person is unique from their physical body.

I decided to test this out. Let's look at this well-known discourse between Jesus and his disciples recorded in the gospel of Matthew. *"Jesus, having come into the regions of Philip's Caesarea, was asking His disciples, saying, **'Who do people say that the Son of Humanity is?'**"* (Matt 16:13)

In the King James Version, this question is rendered as *"Whom do men say that I the Son of Man am?"* This rendering is flawed. While it forms the question in correct grammar, it does not remain true to the way Jesus actually asked the question. In the original scriptures Jesus never once made the claim *"I am the Son of Humanity."* Notice, the question Jesus asked of the disciples was actually, *"Who do people say that the Son of Humanity is?"* Jesus always spoke of his *'Son of Humanity'* identity from the Third Person perspective. He was asking them how did others perceive his human identity.

"And they said, 'Some, John the Baptist.' And others, 'Elijah.' And different ones, 'Jeremiah or one of the prophets.'" (Matt 16:14). The disciples responded, giving the opinions of the Jews. They indicated that Jesus was being compared to other notable Israelite sons of humanity. But now, let us look at the second question that Jesus asked his disciples.

*"But who do you say that **I am**?"* (Matt 16:15). Notice, this question asks for the True Identity, the *'me'*, the *'I'* of Jesus. *"Who do you say that **I am**?"* What was the answer?

Simon Peter said, *"You are **the Christ, the Son of the living God**."* (Matt 16:16). Notice Peter's response. The true identity of Jesus was not the visible man standing before them. The disciples could see Jesus' human identity – the son of Mary, the humble carpenter turned wandering preacher, teacher, healer and prophet. But these were not the *'I'* of Jesus, they were just the roles that he played for a temporary season. These were the assumed aspects of his *'Son of Humanity'* identity. But concerning the true *'me'*, the *'I'* of Jesus, Peter, under heavenly inspiration had exclaimed: *"You are... **the Son of the living God!**"*

That was the real identity of Jesus. The Son of the Living God was a person who was of the realm of the invisible, or spirit realm, which we call heaven. Jesus commended Peter on his observation. He told Peter, *"Blessed are you, Simon Bar Jona! For flesh and blood did not reveal it to you, but My Father in the heavens."* (Matt 16:17). Jesus emphasized that his true identity – *'the Son of God'*, originated not in the *'flesh and blood'* realm of the natural, but from the invisible realm of the spirit, or the heavens. His real identity was who God had declared him to be. Humanity could have declared Jesus to be Son of God, Son of

Man or Son of the Devil. It really did not matter. What mattered was what God had said.

Of himself Jesus declared, *"I came out from, and have come from God."* (John 8:42). I believe that this was the reason why he never equated his *'Son of Humanity'* identity with his *'me'* or *'I'* aspect. He understood that his *'Son of Humanity'* identity was merely a vehicle through which he, the Son of the Living God, could interact with others in this natural realm. The Son of Humanity was the son of Mary, the descendant of David of the tribe of Judah. But these did not comprise his *True Identity*. I could imagine Jesus saying, *"these are not who I am! They are aspects of the Son of Humanity, manifesting in the body that had been prepared for me. My Father has given my true identity to me.* ***I am the Son of the Living God!"***

I give thanks to the Father for the awesome gift of His Son, descending down to humanity so that humanity could ascend up to Him. Is it possible that Jesus' humanity was a pattern for all of us? Could it be that like Jesus, our bodies have been prepared for our *true identity*? Therefore, whenever I stand in front of a mirror, the son of humanity that I see in that reflection, is not *me*, it is not who I am, it is just the body that was prepared for *me*. My humanity could be formed and fashioned into multiple identities that may change every decade, or every year, or even every day. But yet those outward identities are not *me*. They are temporary and transient. I could appear as a king today, and a vagrant tomorrow. But none of those appearances are *me*. What if my true identity – the true *'Me,'* like Jesus' true identity, also has its origin in the invisible realm of the heavens?

Could it be then, that Jesus' role as the *'Son of Humanity'* was more accurately the *'Son of All Humanity?'* In other words, it seems to me that Jesus was the first of many – the prototype – of a new humanity, which like him, would be Sons of God manifested in the flesh. Well then, if that is the case, *who am I?*

CHAPTER 3
I Am Aware that I Am

In this chapter, we will delve a bit deeper into the concepts of the Person and the Personality. We may have experienced our pets' reactions to seeing themselves in a mirror. Or maybe we have seen hilarious videos online of various animals being afraid of their own reflections. Animals do not realize that they are seeing their own reflections in the mirror. This is because they are not *'self-aware.'*

Humanity, however, are the only creatures with a developed sense of self-awareness. Our self-awareness existed before any other aspects of our being. Before our parents taught us our names, we were already self-aware. Before we learned of our genders, ethnicity and nationality, we were self-aware. Our self-awareness was the only knowledge we came into this world with. Every other piece of information that we know, has been given to us from external sources. Our self-awareness is God-given and it is internal. We know that *we are*; you know that *you are*; I know that *I am*.

I *am* reading this book right now. I *am* at a particular location at a particular point in time. I can even project my awareness into the future by planning to be somewhere else tomorrow, or next week, or next month. Jesus acknowledged that his *'Son of Humanity'* identity was the *"body prepared for me."* The *'me'* or the *'I'* was his *true identity*, his self-awareness. When we use the word *'I'*, what are we referring to? *'I'* refers to our self-awareness – our consciousness that *we are existing* and *are aware* of our existence.

» *When we use the word 'I', what are we referring to? 'I' refers to our self-awareness – our consciousness that we are existing and are aware of our existence.*

Close your eyes and say the words *"I am."* As you say those words, use them with the understanding that you are just declaring your existence as a conscious being. You are not saying *what* you are, but just that *you are*. Do not attach any other words to *"I am."* Do not say: *"I am thus"* or *"I am that."* Just simply, *"I am."* By doing this, you are adopting Jesus' understanding. We recall when he said, *"before Abraham was, **I am!**"*

The scripture does not record God breathing the Spirit of Life into any other creature, except humanity. This is why I believe God gave us our self-awareness and ability to self-perceive as part of that Spirit of Life that He breathed into the first man, Adam. This self-awareness, the *'I am'* aspect of us, is therefore a spark of the divine within us. It is what was referred to as the *'spirit within man.'* (1 Cor 2:11). The *'I Am'* self-awareness is the remnant of our God-likeness, for He had declared of Himself, *"I Am Who I Am."* His self-consciousness is what had been breathed into humanity, which gives us our self-awareness, our Person.

Another aspect of our self-awareness is our self-perception. The self-perception is that picture that we have of ourselves, which is not the picture that we see in the mirror, but the picture that we see in our minds. The self-awareness and self-perception are another way of looking at the Person and the Personality. These function in the invisible realm of the Spirit. The picture we see in our minds, which is in the inner spirit (or invisible) realm, motivates and activates the image we see in the mirror, manifesting a particular Personality into the natural realm. As well, our self-perception also influences how we view the external world and others.

Close your eyes and think of yourself. How do you view yourself? Who are you? What is your identity? How do you feel about yourself? Do you think you are smart or dumb, or somewhere in between? Are you handsome and beautiful, or plain, or maybe ugly? Are you worthy or worthless? This mental picture is your self-perception. It is a picture only you can see. It is your own personal concept of yourself. It is who you think you are. The picture in your mind is invisible to all others. It is not so much a picture of physical attributes, but more of a collection of recorded feelings, beliefs, and emotions. Every experience we have had, whether positive or negative, generates an emotion that is linked to that experience. Whenever we think of that experience, we feel that emotion. Some people feel negative emotions when they think of themselves. If they feel unworthy, they experience an emotion that is associated with that unworthiness. All of this occurs invisibly within. That is why it is in the spirit realm. Now open your eyes and look at yourself in the mirror. The image in the mirror is your humanity. This image is not only visible to you, but to all others. This image is in the natural realm. The image in the mirror – your humanity, is the vehicle that brings your self-perception into the visible world.

For the purpose of this book, I will be using the term *'identity'* to mean the spirit within humanity, one's combined self-awareness and self-perception, or their Person and Personality. The Identity is the *'Me'* that Jesus spoke of when he said, *"a body was prepared for Me."* Your Identity is invoked every time you say the word *'I'* or *'me.'* It is quite unique from your humanity. It is the governing aspect of the mind within humanity. It is unique from your gender, ethnicity, height, weight, age, nationality and all the other aspects of your humanity.

Was Jesus' self-awareness and self-perception informed and formed by the opinions of others in his community? Did Jesus get his self-perception from what people told him? Did he view himself according to the numerous opinions around him? It seemed to me that Jesus from a very early age had a certain self-perception, which he openly displayed to his parents. He asked them, *"Did you not know that I had to be in the matters of my Father?"* (Luke 2:49). It is apparent that as a child, Jesus had already seen himself as the Son of the Heavenly Father. He dared to believe that the ancient prophecies had been penned concerning him. It was written, *"Behold, I have come — **in the scroll of the book it is written of me** — to do Your will, O God."* (Heb 10:7). He boldly told the teachers of Jewish religion, *"you search the Scriptures because you think that in them you have eternal life; and **it is they that bear witness about me!**"* (John 5:39)

Jesus was able to find his identity in the scripture. Maybe mine was there too.

CHAPTER 4
Jesus – the Image of the Invisible God

In Paul's epistle to the Colossians, Jesus is described as being *"the image of the invisible God."* (Col 1:15). I do not believe Paul was speaking of the physical attributes of Jesus' humanity. In other words, I do not think that Paul was saying that the invisible God had brown hair, brown eyes, wore fabric clothing and leather sandals. I am understanding Paul to be using the term *'image'* to convey the idea that Jesus was *the visible representative* of the invisible God. This is a concept that is key in understanding the relationship between the invisible and the visible; the Spirit manifests through the Natural; the heavenly manifests through the earthly; the inner manifests through the outer. Jesus' God-likeness – his inner personality, was the personality of his Father. Thus the inner invisible attributes of his Father's personality were manifested through Jesus' outward visible humanity. These traits were outwardly manifested because of Jesus' inner self-awareness and self-perception. His *'Son of Humanity'* identity outwardly radiated what he inwardly believed concerning himself. Thus the invisible *'Son of God'* was made visible through the *'Son of Humanity.'*

Despite Jesus' flawless personality, the people in his community seemed to have had widely varying opinions concerning who he was. Here are some of the broad range of sentiments being bandied about concerning Jesus:

- *"You are a Samaritan and have a demon!"* (John 8:48)

- *"Is this not the son of the carpenter? Is not his mother called Mary, and his brothers James, Joseph, Simon and Judas?"* (Matt 13:55)

- *"A man who was a prophet, mighty in deed and word before God and all the people."* (Luke 24:19)

- *"Never has a man spoken like this, as this man speaks."* (John 7:46)

- *"He has blasphemed."* (Matt 26:65)

- *"He is deserving of death."* (Matt 26:66)

- *"I know who you are, the Holy One of God!"* (Mark 1:24)

- *"Is any good thing able to be out of Nazareth?"* (John 1:46)

- *"You have come from God as a teacher."* (John 3:2)

- *"We found this man misleading our nation, ...he stirs up the people!"* (Luke 23:2,5)

- *"I understand that you are a prophet."* (John 4:19)

- *"This man is not from God."* (John 9:16)

- *"We know that this man is a sinner."* (John 9:24)

If Jesus had been such a person as to internalize these opinions of others concerning who he was, whether their opinions were favorable or not, he would have been a very schizophrenic person! One may also find it strange that there were folks who actually had negative opinions of Jesus. This is not so incredible, when we understand that how we view others largely stems from how we view ourselves. In psychology, there is a term called *'projection.'* People tend to accuse others of what they themselves are guilty of *by projecting their own motives* upon the accused.

What seemed to matter to Jesus however, was what God thought of him. I believe that it was God's opinion of Jesus that informed and formed Jesus' own self-perception. The Gospels give us a peek at what was God's opinion of Jesus' true identity. It was recorded, there came *"a voice out of the cloud saying, 'This is My Son, the beloved, in whom I am well pleased.'"* (Matt 17:5)

Not only did God affirm Jesus' true identity as His Son, but also He praised him as His beloved Son. The Son He loved much, the Son He cherished, treasured, prized and was proud of. What an affirmation! Above anything, children desire the unconditional love and admiration of their parents. Our parents' have a profound influence on the formation of our self-perception. Many psychological issues that plague us as adults, have their foundations laid as a result of emotional trauma that we suffered as children. Hurtful, negative words wound children and paint for them a picture of themselves that lacks worth.

» *Not only did God affirm Jesus' true identity as His Son, but also He praised him as His beloved Son. The Son He loved much, the Son He cherished, treasured, prized and was proud of. What an affirmation!*

The identity of a person is revealed through their visible actions. When someone interacts with us, our behavior paints a visible picture of our person and personality – who we are and what we are like. In other words, people perceive my [invisible] identity through observing my visible actions. What they perceive of my identity is usually in harmony with how I see my [invisible] self. If I see myself as insignificant, without value and unimportant, chances are my personality will manifest in ways that are in harmony with my warped self-perception.

For example, a person who believes that they are without value may overcompensate in their manifested behavior, to be very loud, commanding and brash. They manifest a personality that demands attention. Their self-perception cries out, *"Hey, look at me! Pay attention to me! I am not worthy so I need your attention to make me feel worthy!"*

However, another person, equally believing that they too are without value, may manifest a completely opposite personality. They may appear very withdrawn, extremely shy and unwilling to voice their opinion. Their self-perception cries out, *"DON'T look at me! Don't pay any attention to me! I am not worthy of your attention!"*

In both cases, there is the self-awareness – *"I am."* Both persons are aware of themselves existing. However, their self-perception of their existence is warped. Both believe, *"I am NOT WORTHY."* They have linked their God-given self-awareness – *"I am"* – with an attribute that God never gave them – *"not worthy."*

Now, here is another amazing thing that I discovered. Just as Jesus' self-perception was informed and formed by His Father's opinion of him, so too should my self-perception be informed and formed by God's opinion of Me!

CHAPTER 5
What is God's Image and Likeness?

Created in His Image...

"So God created humanity in his image..." (Gen 1:27)

In my quest to find out God's opinion of me, I decided to go as far back as I could in history to see what was God's opinion of the first members of humanity, Adam and Eve. According to the Biblical narrative, the first humans were made in the image of God. What does it mean that humanity was made in God's image?

Firstly, we need to ascertain how the scriptures used the Hebrew word *'tselem,'* which is rendered as *'image.'* It seems to me that this word was most often associated with carved or molten works depicting the various deities that were worshipped by ancient peoples. These works ranged from tiny figurines to massive statues. Nevertheless, these images were the visible depictions of the imaginations of these people. *These images represented what they imagined their deity looked like.* According to the scriptural use, *the image was the visible manifestation of the invisible imagination.*

Even in the 21st century, many religions still practice making images of their deities. We have various figurines of the Hindu gods – Shiva, Parvati, Krishna, Vishnu, Lakshmi, Ganesh, Nataraja, Devi, Saraswati, Shakti, Buddha, Kali, Murugan, Patanjali and Hanuma. There are various Catholic iconographies of Jesus, Mary and the Saints, all of whom receive veneration. There exists today examples such as the gigantic statue of the Hindu god Bhagavan Hanuman. This statue, located in the village of

Paritala in India, is 135ft (41m) tall! Then there is the statue of Christ the Redeemer in Rio de Janeiro, Brazil. This statue stands at 125ft (38m). All these images are but representations of what the adherents imagined these religious personalities looked like.

When God created humanity *'in His image,'* he was creating man to be a visible representation of Himself. Man is therefore the very proof that an invisible God exists. The apostle Paul confirmed, *"For **His invisible attributes**, namely, his eternal power and divine nature, **have been clearly perceived**, ever since the creation of the world, **in the things that have been made**..."* (Rom 1:20). This is another application of the spiritual principle of the invisible manifesting through the visible. ***Humanity was the visible form prepared for the purpose of manifesting the invisible God.***

Created according to His Likeness

When religious adherents fashioned their deities who were thought to have supernatural powers, a wooden, stone or metal statue could never have done justice to that which had been imagined! No matter how immense, intricately designed, or ornately detailed these images were, they still were less than the glory that they had in their creator's imagination. When all was said and done, they are still wood, stone and metal objects.

However, unlike the countless images made by men, God invested into His image the Spirit of Life! The Bible narrative tells us, *"And the LORD God formed humanity of the dust of the ground, and breathed into his nostrils the **Spirit of Life**; and man became a living being."* (Gen 2:7). According to the narrative, humanity was made from the dust of the ground, or the elements of the earth, just like all other images were made from the elements of the earth. The difference with God's image was that He placed within that image, the Spirit of Life. What is the Spirit of Life? If we are consistent, we can say that the Spirit of Life is the Spirit that gives Life. It is that which brings about the Life within.

I believe that this Life is not just the ability to live. I believe the essence of this Life is the ability, like God, to be Self-Aware and to Self-Perceive. I believe this is what God meant when he said, *"Let us make humanity in our image, according to our likeness..."* (Gen 1:26). I believe this is so because, as I indicated earlier, it was only humanity that God gave this Spirit of Life. He did not give it to the animals. They have life, but not the Likeness of God.

» *I believe that this Life is not just the ability to live, I believe the essence of this Life is the ability, like God, to be Self-Aware and to Self-Perceive. I believe this is what God meant when he said, "Let us make humanity in our image, according to our likeness..."*

So, I began to see that God not only made humanity in His image, but also according to His likeness. This is the aspect of Himself that He placed in us that was actually *like* Him! At the instant when humanity was fashioned in the image of God from the dust of the ground, it was like all other images. It could not speak, hear, nor think. It was just an image made from the elements of the earth. It might just as well have been a cadaver. There was no life in it, neither spirit, nor personality, nor intelligence! It was only when God placed the Spirit of Life in the image that humanity became a living being. This image was made of the elements of the earth – like all other images. However, unlike other images, it contained the likeness of God – a Living Spirit! God's Spirit of Life was His invisible Likeness, which would manifest through the visible image or body. I can therefore conclude that a

21

living being is a combination of spirit and body. The spirit is the invisible intangible aspect, which came from God. It governs the thoughts, feelings and emotions. It is the identity. The body is the visible physical aspect of humanity, it came from the elements of the earth. The spirit and the body interact to reveal the person and the personality.

In the Gospels, Jesus is quoted as saying, *"God is Spirit..."* (John 4:24). God is spirit and therefore His likeness must also be spirit. At this point, I think it would be helpful to look briefly at what has been revealed to us in the scripture concerning the spirit.

God is Spirit

The original words that Bibles render as *'spirit'* are the Hebrew *'ruach'* and *'neshamah'*, and the Greek *'pneuma.'* All these words convey the sense of breath, air and wind. These natural phenomena were metaphors used to describe God. Breath, wind and air, like spirit, are invisible to the human eye. However, the movement of wind and air can be discerned in the swaying of the trees, and in the disturbance of the leaves. Likewise, spirit is invisible, but can be discerned in the internal movements within humanity. My understanding of spirit as it applies to the Father, is that it speaks of the 'Who' (person of God), which manifests the 'How' (personality of God) through the 'What' (form/nature of God).

The Person of God

The person of God identifies *'Who is God.'* The use of the word *'God'* in this context speaks of the One True Living God – the Father of all. It is interesting how God referred to Himself when communing with Moses. He said, *"I Am Who I Am..."* (Ex 6:14).

Here God employs self-awareness, *"I Am."* God declares that He is conscious of His existence, however, since He is the Father, then He Himself *is* Consciousness and *the Source of* Consciousness. He Himself is Life and the source of Life. He is Love, Joy, Wisdom and Power. The scripture says He is "th*e immortal, invisible, ...God*..." (1Tim 1:17). These all are not tangible things, they are a combined invisible Intelligence that we call 'God.' Being inherently invisible therefore, the person of God is Spirit.

The Personality of God

The personality of God reveals *'How is God'* like. His personality comprises those invisible qualities that radiate out from Him toward us. *His Personality reveals His Person – 'Who I Am'* – through many varied providential encounters we experience from day to day. God gives life. He gives joy, He heals and He loves. He gives wisdom and He empowers us. But *"No one has ever yet seen God..."* (John 1:18) – He is invisible, so also is His Personality. Therefore the personality of God is also Spirit.

The Form of God

The form or nature of God addresses the *'What is God's manifested form.'* He has no definite form like humanity. Moses reminded the Israelites that, *"all of you saw **no manner of embodiment** on the day that the LORD spoke unto you in Horeb out of the midst of the fire..."* (Deut 4:15). He has neither body nor body parts. Jesus had said, *"...spirit does not have flesh and bones..."* (Luke 24:39). He is not constrained in space and time. Solomon said of God, *"...behold, heaven and the heaven of heavens **cannot contain you**; how much less this house which I have built!"* (2Chr 6:18).

Some may object, since in the scriptures, God is depicted with human features. In some places He is described as having white hair, sitting on a throne, riding chariots, etc. This is however what is called the *'Anthropomorphism of God.'* Anthropomorphism essentially is the depiction of God in a human-like form, to help humanity to better understand what God wanted to communicate at that time. For example, according to the narrative, Moses received two tablets of the Ten Commandments inscribed by *'the finger of God.'* Do we suppose that a giant finger came from heaven to etch the words onto the stone tablets? Consider how Jesus understood the concept of the *'finger of God.'* He told the Jews, *"...I cast out the demons by **the finger of God**..."* (Luke 11:20). We see that it is more likely that the *'finger of God'* was a Hebrew idiom referring to the *'power of God.'*

While God Himself is not visible to the natural eye, He manifests through the beings He has created. We are told that, *"...by Him were all things created, that are in heaven, and that are in earth, **visible and invisible**, whether they be thrones, or dominions, or principalities, or powers: **all things were created by Him, and for Him**..."* (Col 1:16).

According to the scripture, there are visible and invisible created beings; humanity is visible, and the angelic beings are mostly invisible to us. Both the visible and invisible creatures are agencies through which God manifests Himself. We experience the joy He gives, we receive His healing, we bask in His love, through the visible creation and sometimes from within ourselves. Thus we may encounter God's Person manifesting His love to us when our loved one gives us a hug and a kiss. We experience God's Joy through happy experiences of receiving gifts from others. We experience God's protection through tiny daily deliverances, which we may not even be aware of. We are told, *"For **His invisible attributes**, namely, his eternal power and divine nature, **have been clearly perceived**, ever since the creation of the world, **in the**</*

things that have been made..." (Rom 1:20). Humanity as God's creation (*the things that have been made*) are the manifested evidence of an invisible God. The invisible manifests through the visible. Our intelligence, capacity to love, create, design, judge and be self-aware, are all invisible attributes from God. These invisible spiritual characteristics flow from God's person. Thus we can conclude that the form of God is not fixed. He manifests *through and in* His Creation.

Humanity's Person and Personality are Spirit

Like God, humanity has several aspects. There is the *'Who'* (individual person), which the *'How'* (individual personality) manifests through the *'What'* (form/nature of humanity). Similar to God, *humanity's person and personality are spirit*, they are all intangible, invisible attributes. Similar to God, our *'Who'* person is our *'I am,'* our own self-awareness. However, unlike God, *humanity's form is restricted to the physical body*. Humanity's form is the earthly biological body, composed of the elements of the earth.

All the intangible aspects of humanity are attributed to the spirit within humanity. The apostle indicated, *"For who among men knows the things of humanity, **except the spirit of humanity within him?"** (1Cor 2:11). Humanity, according to the scripture, has a spirit within. That spirit comprises the person and their personality. The scripture refers to the spirit of a person as the *"inner man..."* (2 Cor 4:16). This *'spirit'* of the *'person'* governs the thoughts and feelings, which comprise the *'personality.'* This personality then manifests the person through the actions of the body. A happy spirit shows in the little dance of the limbs and the bright smile in the face of *a happy person*. It is important to grasp that anything that is spirit originates in the invisible realm, being first *'seen'* in the mind or experienced in the *'inner man.'* For example, Joy cannot be seen, it wholly originates in the spirit realm of the mind and is experienced in the *'inner man.'* However, most times it is allowed to manifest – made visible and tangible – through actions of the body.

God communicates with the spirit that is within humanity. Humanity manifests the personality of God when they love unconditionally, when they advocate for life and when they act in wisdom. It is also in the realm of the spirit that God effects positive change within humanity. Thus the likeness that God placed within humanity was that self-awareness, that we too like God can say, *"I Am."*

Now, how does all this help me in the quest for my identity? At the creation, God created humanity in His Image, as a living being bearing His Likeness. What was God's opinion of humanity at that time? If I could discover what was God's opinion of humanity at creation, then maybe I would also discover what is God's opinion of me – a son of humanity.

CHAPTER 6
I have said, 'You are Gods!'

At the creation, humanity came to life after receiving the Spirit of Life. Of humanity at that time it was written *"You have made him a little less than God, and have crowned him with glory and honor..."* (Ps 8:5). Depending on which Bible translation you have, this verse may be rendered as *'a little lower than the angels.'* However, the word rendered as *'angels'* in this verse, is the very same word *'elohim'* which is normally rendered as *'God'* or *'Gods.'*

I did some research on the word *'elohim'* and I found out some very eye-opening information. Firstly, this word could be singular or plural depending on whether the verb or adjective it governs is singular or plural. In other words, in the original Hebrew scripture, if *'elohim'* governs a singular verb, then it is a singular noun, and should be understood as a single one – *'God.'* If *'elohim'* governs a plural verb, then it is a plural noun, and should be understood as several in number – *'Gods.'* English Bibles have traditionally capitalized *'God'* if the context is speaking of the Father, the One True God.

However, the Hebrew writers also sometimes used the same word *'elohim'* when referring to other beings, such as religious deities, angels and even people. It seems therefore that this word carries with it the idea of beings possessing great power, intellect and influence. According to the scripture, the Father, the creator and live-giver, *"is greater than all Gods [elohim]: for in the thing wherein they dealt proudly He was above them."* (Exod 18:11).

> » *The Hebrew writers also sometimes used the same word 'elohim' when referring to other beings, such as religious deities, angels and even people. It seems therefore that this word carries with it the idea of beings possessing great power, intellect and influence.*

The point that I wish to bring to the reader's attention however, is that the term *'God'* was not unique to the divine all-powerful, all-knowing One, but it was a generic term used for superior beings. In this book, I will render the singular title *'elohim'* as *'God'* to refer to the One True Living God, who was revealed to us by His Son Jesus as *'The Father.'* This is in harmony with the apostle Paul who declared: *"...there are many Gods and many lords, **yet to us there is one God the Father**, of whom are all things, and we for Him; and one Lord, Jesus Christ, by whom are all things, and we through him..."* (1Cor 8:5-6). For the plural instances of *'elohim,'* I will use the plural title of *'Gods.'*

Thus, according to Psalm 8:5, humanity at the creation were a junior class of Gods, they were created *a little less* than God. What was it that qualified them to be identified as Gods? Was it the elements of the earth? Or was it the Spirit of Life within? I believe it was the Spirit of Life – the likeness of God, within them. The likeness had been given directly from God. He had breathed His own Spirit of Life into humanity. The Spirit of Life was that which made them God-like. It was the Spirit of Life that gave them their True Identity.

In the book of John, Jesus startled the religious leaders of his day with this zinger: *"Is it not written in your Law: **'I said you are Gods'**?"* (John 10:34). Jesus was quoting from the Jewish Law or Torah, the written scriptures consisting of the writings of Moses, the prophets and the Psalms. In the 82nd Psalm, God is quoted as saying, *"I have said, '**All of you are Gods**; and all of* *you are **children of the Most High.**'"* (Ps 82:6)

Jesus was at the time responding to the religious leaders' outrage at his claim of being the Son of God. Jesus answered them by appealing to the Jewish scriptures. He pointed out that God had already set the precedent by calling sons of humanity, Gods. Jesus then pointed out that he had not even gone as far as the Father had. He had not said that he was God or a God. He had simply said he was the Son of God.

I know many Christians have at the least, a reluctance, and at the most, a fear, of even addressing what Jesus and the scriptures say on this matter. But I believe that Jesus was hinting at my true identity.

I took the time to layout what Jesus said on this matter, as well as the scripture in the Psalm that he referenced.

- *"God called them 'Gods' to whom the word of God came."* (John 10:35)

- *"All of you are Gods; and all of you are children of the Most High."* (Ps 82:6)

- *"All of you shall die like men, and fall like one of the princes."* (Ps 82:7)

Assuming that all of the above claims were true, then I can reason that in God's opinion, the sons of humanity to whom the word of God came were 'Gods.' They were called Gods since they were the children of the Most High God. However, because they were also sons of humanity, they were subject to death. I can deduce from this, that sons of humanity, to whom the Word of God came, were a class of Gods. But since humanity's form was made of the elements of the earth, whenever those elements return to the earth, these Gods experience death. It also seems that God was saying that the Word of God was capable of restoring humanity to its lofty status as Gods, as they were at the creation.

We have already seen that at the creation, God breathed into humanity the Spirit of Life. We saw that this Spirit was what endowed humanity with the likeness of God. We see that at creation, humanity was made as a junior class of Gods.

Now, according to John 10:35, those to whom the Word of God came, God had called them Gods. When I thought upon this, I began to see what was meant. The Word of God is actually God's thoughts breathed into humanity. God's thoughts originate within Himself. God's thoughts are like Him – Spirit, they are His Likeness. Thus, the Word of God (His Spirit) was breathed out and received into humanity, just as at the creation. What happened at the creation when God breathed the Spirit of Life into humanity? It was recorded that humanity became a junior class of Gods. I am beginning to see a principle. Whenever humanity received the Word of God (God's Spirit), the likeness of God was manifested in humanity.

Consequently Jesus, as recorded in John 10:35, is reasoning on the same principle. He said, *"He called them Gods to whom the Word of God came,"* (John 10:35). Therefore it is apparent to me that the reception of the Opinion of God is essential for the reproduction in humanity of His likeness, by which humanity can be called Gods.

In summary, we have learned that according to God's Opinion:

- At the creation, humanity possessed God's Spirit of Life within, and were a class of Gods.

- Humanity to whom the Word of God (God's Spirit) came, were called Gods.

- The reception of the Word of God (God's Spirit), facilitates the likeness of God within, creating Gods out of humanity.

Humanity's identity as Gods was never mentioned to me in all of my religious education. I had no idea of humanity's divine heritage. Could it be that my true identity could be found in this divine origin? In my quest to find out who I am, I will attempt to ascertain how this heritage had informed and formed humanity's self-awareness and self-perception at the creation.

CHAPTER 7
Humanity's Identity had been Informed and Formed by God's Opinion

Do you remember how I had realized that my self-awareness and self-perception had been informed and formed by a combination of others' opinions of me? I now understand that God's original intention was, and still is, that humanity's self-awareness and self-perception was to be informed and formed only by God's opinion, and not any other.

At the creation, humanity was in a loving trusting relationship with God. Jesus did say, *"this is eternal life, **that they may know You**, the only true God..."* (John 17:3). Eternal life as God defined it, was an intimate love relationship with Him. God demonstrated love to humanity by providing bountifully. The Garden of Eden was evidence of God's Love. Everything was already provided for humanity. *"And out of the ground made the LORD God to grow **every tree that is pleasant to the sight, and good for food**..."* (Gen 2:9). Notice God provided not a few trees, but *every* tree that is good for food. This was God's loving abundant provision for humanity. Also recall that we had read the words of the psalmist concerning humanity, *"You have made him a little less than God, and have crowned him with glory and honor..."* (Ps 8:5). God had favored humanity with glory and honor. He had bestowed upon them praise-worthy splendor and nobility.

With reference to humanity's emotional well-being, the psalmist testified *"...in Your presence is fullness of joy; at Your right hand there are pleasures for evermore,"* (Ps 16:11). This lets us know that humanity felt emotionally fulfilled in God's presence. They did not feel condemned, unworthy, unloved, distrusted nor cheated in any way. Instead, their experience was one of perfect delight. They could feel free to be themselves, Gods in the presence of God. Thus, humanity's spirit aspect – their self-awareness and self-perception – was first informed by God's loving opinion of them.

Since God was loving and trustworthy, humanity felt loved and safe. God's love and trust toward them formed their self-awareness, *'We are God's beloved children, His delight.'* They were aware that God loved them and that He was honest with them. That awareness informed their self-perception that they too were worthy and trustworthy. In response they loved God and loved each other. As the apostle John many millennia later wrote, *"we love Him, **because He first loved us**, ...he who loves God loves his brother also..."* (1John 4:19,21).

» *They were aware that God loved them and that He was honest with them. That awareness informed their self-perception that they too were worthy and trustworthy. In response they loved God and loved each other.*

God's abundant provision for them made them aware that they lacked nothing. They felt secure and abundant, which in turn made them confident and generous. God's favor towards them resulted in them being aware of their worth and value in His estimation of them. This in turn manifested graciousness and kindness from them toward God and each other. I believe that humanity remained in the presence of God because their self-awareness and self-perception had been perfectly formed and informed by His Opinion of them. They were His image, manifesting His likeness.

From these insights, I can see that something terrible must have happened to cause humanity to lose sight of God's opinion. Humanity today no longer seems to be aware of God's opinion. People's self-awareness and self-perception seem to be very warped.

Even among the various religions, which claim to be teaching about God, there seems to be the doctrine that mankind is not worthy of an offended God's love, favor, honor nor esteem. In fact the Bibles render the Greek word *'charis'* as the English word *'grace.'* Grace carries the implication that the receiver thereof is an unworthy wretch to whom God extends pardon when their actions are reformed. I think that the word *'grace'* is not the best rendering of *'charis.'* It seems to me *'grace'* is somehow humanity's flawed perspective, while *'charis'* is God's true perspective. *'Charis'* has more to do with *God's innate non-stop abundant overflowing loving-kindness.* God just pours out *'charis'* wherever and to whomever. It is who He is – *Love.* It is not the 'sinner' who moves God to extend grace by his repentance. It is God's loving-kindness that causes the sinner to change, not just the actions, but also their identity! Adam and Eve were created to be recipients of God's non-stop loving-kindness, His *'charis.'* God reaches out to humanity *because of Who He is and How He is* – His Person and Personality of *'Charis!'*

Christians seem to have a sort of schizophrenic view of God. At one time He is Love, then another time he seemed to have been quite fine with exterminating whole families and tribes of ancient people. We may have heard Christians giving the 'good news' of a God who is so loving that he condemns those who rejected Him to roast in hell-fire, sometimes for short periods, sometimes for eternity, depending on the particular denomination's version of the 'gospel.'

It seems to me that Christians have not considered the fact that humanity had chosen the paradigm of the Tree of Knowledge of Good and Evil. Under this paradigm, humanity had lost sight of God's true character and had ceased to trust in Him. As a result, His true character became an enigma, due to humanity's distorted perception of Him. It is only when humanity receives God's true opinion of themselves, that they begin to see clearly that God is not evil, nor is He vicious, as the Old Scriptures seem to portray Him. The truth about God's opinion of humanity is that *"He is full of affection and is compassionate"* toward us. (Jas 5:11)

I strongly believe that a person's idea of God's opinion of humanity directly affects that person's identity. If their idea of God's opinion is distorted, they would be like the waves tossed to and fro – a restless soul, never able to have peace within. Anyone who is comfortable with their God executing such unprecedented violence against humanity, would themselves likely to be indifferent toward the sufferings of humanity, and may even be prone to exhibiting and receiving violence themselves.

Since it was God's plan that humanity's self-awareness and self-perception was to be informed and formed by His opinion, then if that opinion was ever to be misconstrued, misinterpreted, or even distorted, humanity's self-awareness and self-perception would likewise be corrupted.

This is what I believe happened during humanity's encounter with the Adversary in the Garden of Eden. Humanity chose to eat from the Tree of the Knowledge of Good and Evil because the adversary had succeeded in getting humanity to believe in a corrupt report of God's opinion of them.

Maybe I could learn from that encounter some valuable information that would help me in my quest in discovering my true identity.

CHAPTER 8
The Fall from the Likeness

According to the Bible narrative, humanity had chosen to eat from the Tree of Knowledge of Good and Evil, instead of the Tree of Life.

The Tree of Knowledge of Good and Evil had always been an enigma to me. God had said that humanity should not eat from this tree. God had warned them, *"but of the tree of the knowledge of good and evil, you shall not eat of it;* ***for in the day that you eat of it you will surely die."*** (Gen 2:17). According to God, humanity would die in the very day that they ate the forbidden fruit. Yet when humanity did eat of that tree, it seems to me that they did not instantly die. In fact, Adam is recorded to have lived on to an age of 930 years. This tells me that the *'death'* that God warned about was not referring to the return of the elements of the body back to the earth.

I am seeing that the *'death'* that God warned about, would have to be related to the Spirit of Life that had been placed in humanity. In other words, this *'death'* was connected to a corruption of the Likeness of God. This *'death'* happened the instant humanity partook of that tree. I believe that this death was as a result of the corruption of the Likeness of God. It is a consequence of the degradation of the Spirit of Life within humanity. This *'death'* is the end-product of humanity's corrupted self-awareness and self-perception. Remember, self-awareness and self-perception were given through the Spirit of Life. The identity is composed of the self-awareness and self-perception. If there was a degradation of the Likeness of God within humanity, it would be seen in a degradation or corruption of humanity's self-awareness and self-perception. In turn, this corruption would lead humanity to separate themselves from God, who was their source of Life. *A choice to separate from Life is a choice to unite with Death!* In effect, humanity chose *eternal death* because of the corruption of their self-awareness and self-perception.

» *I am seeing that the 'death' that God warned about, would have to be related to the Spirit of Life that had been placed in humanity. In other words, this 'death' was connected to a corruption of the Likeness of God.*

Can we ascertain the corruption of humanity's identity from the Bible? I believe we can. Let's look at the Biblical narrative of the fall of humanity.

The Bible narrative called our attention to two trees out of all the trees that God had placed in the garden. *"And out of the ground made the LORD God to grow every tree that is pleasant to the sight, and good for food; the **Tree Of Life** also in the midst of the garden, and the **Tree Of Knowledge Of Good And Evil**."* (Gen 2:9)

The two trees were significant of the ways humanity could relate to God. The Tree of Life was the way of Life, it represented the relationship to God that humanity had been created in, and the identity that humanity had been created with. They were created as Gods with an abundantly favored, honored and esteemed status in the joyful presence of a loving Father. They had only to rest in that Life and in God's Opinion of them. I believe this was what the Tree of Life symbolized.

*"And the LORD God commanded the man, saying, '**Of every tree of the garden you may freely eat: but of the Tree of the Knowledge of Good and Evil, you shall not eat of it: for in the day that you eat thereof you shall surely die.**'"* (Gen 2:16-17)

Eating from the Tree of the Knowledge of Good and Evil however, was forbidden. The consequence of eating from this tree was death. This tree then, was the antithesis of the Tree of Life. The name of this tree also, gave some indication of what it represented. What is the Knowledge of Good and Evil? It is Morality. It is knowledge of Right and Wrong. This tree was the way of all religion, the teaching of what is morally right and wrong. These two trees in the Garden, were juxtaposed to illustrate two distinct ways that humanity could choose to relate to God.

- One, by receiving God's opinion (the Tree of Life);

- The other, by moral laws (the Tree of the Knowledge of Good and Evil).

However, God warned humanity that the way of the Tree of the Knowledge of Good and Evil was death. That death would essentially be the opposite of what humanity already had. In other words, they already had an abundantly favored, honored and esteemed life in the joyful presence of a loving Father. If they chose the Tree of the Knowledge of Good and Evil, they would be rejecting the abundance, the favor, the esteem, the joy and the identity as children of the Most High. Their self-awareness and self-perception would no longer be formed and informed by God's opinion, but by a distorted perception of God.

Let's follow the narrative and see how this was manifested.

According to the Bible narrative, the serpent was portrayed as enticing humanity to eat of the forbidden tree by striking at the very foundation of their identity. First came the subtle hint that God was not being abundantly generous to them. The serpent is recorded as enquiring, *"Has God really said, 'You **shall not eat of any tree** of the garden?'"* (Gen 3:1). Within the question resides the accusation of restriction, scarcity and lack. *'Why has God forbidden you from eating from **all of these trees**? Why has*

He restricted your freedom, and prevented you from abundance?'
While this question may seem ridiculous on the surface, it is a
sinister way to implant a thought in the mind. For example, if I
say to you, *'have you seen a purple banana?'* The question immediately causes you to think of a purple banana. The question
implants the thought into your mind. Whether you actually saw
a purple banana or not, is irrelevant; you have already pictured
it in your mind.

Likewise, the question caused the woman to think of God forbidding them to eat from all the trees. The issue was not whether this
was true or not, the serpent's intent was to get her mind thinking about what the question surmised. Then as the mind ponders
on the question, the thoughts would follow through logically. *'If
God does not want us to eat from all these trees, then that means
He is really not generous. Why is He not generous? Maybe it's
because we are not worthy of His generosity. Why are we not
worthy of His generosity? Probably it's because we are made of
the dust of the ground.'* Do you see how the instant that humanity's self-awareness became informed by a distorted perception
of God, its self-perception was immediately affected?

The woman's response to the serpent's question was a little too
fervent. She insisted, *"Of the fruit of the trees of the garden we
may eat, but of the fruit of the tree which is in the middle of the
garden, God has said, 'You shall not eat of it, **neither shall you
touch it**, lest you die.'"* (Gen 3:2-3). Notice she overcompen-
sated in her reply. She insisted that God had said that the tree
was not to be touched. This was not so. God only forbade *eating*
from the tree. God had said nothing about *touching* the tree. This
is how I can deduce that the first question was doing its intended
work. The fact that the woman was willing to defend God from
the false allegation by over-stating his sole restriction shows that
she had indeed considered the idea that had been implanted by

the question.

Following up on this devious query, the enemy whispered, *"You* ***won't*** *surely die!"* (Gen 3:4). This assertion was loaded with poison. Without directly stating it, the implication of this falsehood was that God had lied to humanity. The woman may have reasoned, *'why would God lie to us? Maybe it is because He doesn't trust us. Maybe it is because we are not worthy of His trust.'*

The serpent sensed that the woman was then vulnerable. He struck with deadly precision, *"for God knows that in the day you eat it, your eyes will be opened,* ***and you will be like Gods...****"* (Gen 3:5). This deceiving lie was the most damaging, calculated attack on humanity's self-awareness and self-perception to date!

Firstly, by stating that *'God knows,'* the insinuation was made that God had an ulterior and sinister motive for forbidding humanity from eating of the tree. *'God* ***knows*** *there is a blessing contained in this fruit, but He doesn't want you to obtain it!'* The implication was that God had withheld the best from humanity. The suggestion was that God didn't want humanity to have a truly abundant life. This in turn impacted their self-perception. Feelings of discontentment stirred within. *'How could God be so selfish?'* Then the desire came to seek for this *'blessing'* through alternative means. *'Maybe we can obtain the blessing by eating the fruit!'* This was the seed of self-sufficiency being planted in humanity's self-awareness. *'I am self-sufficient, I can do it without God!'*

This was followed by the devilish fabrication that their eyes would be opened after eating the fruit. This implied that their eyes had been shut all the while, that in reality they had been in darkness and wretched ignorance. This falsehood made God seem like a deceiver, and a slave-master, who desired only blind obedience of the ignorant and foolish. This in turn impacted their self-perception. They perceived themselves as deceived, ignorant and foolish. Feelings of rebellion against this slave-master began to swell within.

And lastly came the deadliest poison, that by partaking of the forbidden tree, *'you will be like Gods...'* Of all the attacks that the enemy had made on humanity, this one lets me know that his target was man's self-awareness and self-perception. Hadn't humanity already been made in the likeness of God? Why then should humanity need to eat of the forbidden tree to be like Gods, when they already were?

The fact that humanity proceeded to partake of the forbidden tree after being convinced by the serpent, indicates to me that the adversary had succeeded in corrupting their self-awareness and self-perception. They then perceived themselves as being not like God. Instead of trusting in God's opinion of them, they began to view themselves from a corrupted self-awareness and self-perception. They now believed that they needed to make themselves be like God!

> » *Hadn't humanity already been made in the likeness of God? Why then should humanity need to eat of the forbidden tree to be like Gods, when they already were?*

And so, as the narrative indicated, humanity partook of the Tree of the Knowledge of Good and Evil. They submitted themselves to the paradigm of having a self-awareness that was divorced from God. Humanity no longer bore the likeness of God, because they stopped believing that they were like God. They now believed that they needed to accumulate moral knowledge *to become like God*. They believed that they needed to follow a moral list of Good and Evil Do's and Don'ts to attain to God-likeness and to come into God's favor. Meanwhile they perceived God as not being worthy of their trust. As a result of this corrupted self-perception they neither could trust each other. They perceived God as withholding from them abundant life and His abundant generosity. Therefore, they strove to obtain these by their own strength and ingenuity. As a result of this corrupted self-perception they believed that they needed to independently provide for themselves, and they became selfish and lacking.

Everything of God became perceived as being out of the reach of humanity. The self-awareness of humanity has to this day been based on that false premise. In fact, this is most portrayed in the major religions of the world as they *'confess'* their wretched unworthiness, thinking that they are appeasing an offended God who delights in the abasement of humanity. Today's belief that we may bring ourselves into favor with God by our diligent observance of moral lists of Good and Evil Do's and Don'ts, stems from humanity's corrupted self-awareness and self-perception. The apostle wrote. *"For all have missed the mark, and come short of the glory of God...."* (Rom 3:23).

It is essential to note that the word that many Bibles have rendered as *'sin,'* has in the original language the meaning *'to miss the mark.'* Most religions today have relegated the solution of humanity's fallen condition to the following of a moral list of Good and Evil Do's and Don'ts. But according to God, humanity has missed the mark by falling short of the glory that He had created them with. That mark is not found in the Tree of the Knowledge of Good and Evil, but in the Tree of Life.

I believe that the mark that we have missed is an identity that is informed and formed by God's opinion. Any less, and we have missed the mark. The *'death'* that humanity suffers from is not the return of the biological body to the elements of the ground. As we have seen, the biological body is merely a vessel that God prepared for the True Identity. The *'death'* that afflicts humanity is caused by *the refusal to believe God's true opinion of them.* This refusal results in humanity harboring an irrational dread of being in God's presence.

After partaking of the forbidden fruit, Adam and Eve experienced this severe dread. Their 'eyes' – their self-perception and self-awareness – were now changed. Instead of perceiving God as their loving Father, He now seemed to them now as an angry judge intent on their destruction. Instead of experiencing fullness of joy and eternal pleasures in God's presence, they experienced extreme terror. In panic, they sought to hide themselves from Him.

Adam told God, *"I heard your voice in the garden, and **I was afraid**, because I was naked; and **I hid myself**..."* (Gen 3:10). Instead of feeling loved and accepted, they now experienced Fear and Shame. What had changed? Had God's opinion of humanity changed? Did He stop loving them? Had He uttered one word of condemnation? No, God had not changed, neither had His opinion changed. It was humanity's opinion of God and the paradigm of their relationship to Him, that had changed. Why did humanity's opinion of God change? It changed because *humanity believed that God had changed His opinion of them.* The paradigm of humanity's relationship to God had also changed. They had chosen the way of the Tree of the Knowledge of Good and Evil, and now the effects of that paradigm were being made manifest to them.

God's True Character was now obscured from humanity. The paradigm of the Tree of the Knowledge of Good and Evil was a paradigm of perfect works and performance in an attempt to climb out of humanity's curse of *'death.'* Yet God knew that this way was unfruitful. He sadly told humanity, *"cursed is the ground because of you; in pain you shall eat of it all the days of your life;* **thorns and thistles it shall bring forth for you...** *By the sweat of your face you shall eat bread,* **till you return to the ground, for out of it you were taken...**" (Gen 3:17-19). God had to allow humanity's choice to play out. Therefore, humanity was put under the dominion of death. As the apostle revealed, *"for the wages of sin is death..."* (Rom 6:23). Indeed, the reward for missing the mark, is the separation from God that humanity chose.

Humanity's death was as a result of their choice to remain *separated from God.* As long as humanity remains separated from God, their inner spirit remains defective. Yet that choice is largely due to the corrupt report of God's Character that has been passed down to us. That corrupt report seems validated by the paradigm of the Tree of the Knowledge of Good and Evil. The fact remains that mankind cannot have eternal life while being separated from the Source of Life! The distorted view of God causes humanity to being willing to do *"all that He commands,"* yet not be willing to love and trust Him. *"Do not let God speak to us, lest we die!"* (Exod 20:19).

It is only whenever humanity should believe in God's True Opinion of them, then that choice would result in them seeing Him for who He really is, and the fear of Him would be removed. Once the terror of God is removed and replaced with love for Him, then humanity would cling to God and desire to be one with Him. This oneness would unite His Spirit to theirs, resulting in eternal life. This is humanity's *'resurrection.'*

In my search for my true identity, I must therefore discover God's opinion of me, and embrace it.

CHAPTER 9
Humanity Restored In Christ

*"So also it has been written, 'The first man Adam became a living soul.' **The last Adam** became **a life-giving spirit.**"* (1Cor 15:45)

According to the Holy Spirit inspired apostle Paul, Jesus was the *'last Adam'* and a *'Life-Giving Spirit.'* This is significant. The first Adam was the father of humanity. Because of Adam's fall, all of humanity inherited a defective spirit due to a corrupt identity. It is more correct to say that Adam became the father of a fallen humanity. I believe that Adam passed on the corrupt opinion of humanity to his children, and they to their children's children. That corrupt opinion is reinforced by the paradigm of the Tree of the Knowledge of Good and Evil. It causes humanity to distrust God. It paints God as being distant and removed from humanity. God is perceived as against humanity, intent on humanity's destruction and generally unconcerned about humanity, while simultaneously demanding absolute pinpoint obedience to copious lists of Do's and Don'ts. However, let us remember that all of this is a misconception of God's true opinion. This misconception was as a result of humanity's choice of the Tree of the Knowledge of Good and Evil. God never changed His opinion toward humanity. It was humanity's opinion about God that changed.

This misinformed belief about God's opinion of humanity, in turn formed humanity's self-perception of being of little value to God except as hard-working slaves, whose sole goal is to please God by perpetual endeavors to achieve flawless observance of the lists of Do's and Don'ts. Humanity is viewed as having to provide for themselves, because God is not bothered with such menial things. In turn man becomes very selfish and withholds from others, just as he views God as withholding from him.

This distrustful view of God caused humanity to be fearful of Him, separating themselves from Him. That separation leads to death.

Jesus, however, was another Adam, meaning that he, like the first Adam, is the head of a new seed of humanity. This new seed, unlike the seed from the first Adam, has been given the True opinion of God to correctly inform and form humanity's identity. In fact, in this new seed is Christ himself. Just as in nature, a seed contains a fully grown fruit-bearing tree, so too Christ is the Promised Seed, containing in himself the ability to reproduce himself in countless earthen vessels of humanity.

Christ is the *'Life-giving Spirit,'* indicating that humanity's problem was a defective spirit, or inner man. As a result of humanity believing the corrupt report about God, they became terrified of Him and fled from His presence. This disconnected them from His Life, and as a result the Spirit of Life that had been first breathed into humanity became corrupted. God solved this problem by providing a *'new Spirit,'* which is Christ. Receiving Christ results in the restoration of the likeness of God in the believer. This makes Jesus *'the Way'* (for Humanity's Correct Identity), *'the Truth'* (of God's Opinion of Humanity) and *'the Life'* (which had been rejected by the First Adam).

» *Christ is the 'Life-giving Spirit,' indicating that humanity's problem was a defective spirit, or inner man. The Spirit of Life first breathed into humanity had become corrupted. God solved this problem by providing a 'new Spirit,' which is Christ.*

Let's see how Jesus (the Son of Humanity) bore the same traits that Adam (the head of humanity) had before the fall.

Image of God

- Adam: *"So God created humanity **in His own image...**"* (Gen 1:27)

- Jesus: *"...Christ, who is **the image of God...**"* (2Cor 4:4)

Likeness of God

- Adam: *"...God formed humanity, **in the likeness of God**, He made him..."* (Gen 5:1)

- Jesus: *"The one having **seen me has seen the Father...**"* (John 14:9)

Made a little lower than God

- Adam: *"For you have made him **a little lower than God...**"* (Ps 8:5)

- Jesus: *"But we see Jesus, who was **made a little lower than God** for the suffering of death..."* (Heb 2:9)

Crowned with glory and honor

- Adam: *"For you ...have **crowned him with glory and honor.**"* (Ps 8:5)

- Jesus: *"But we see Jesus ...**crowned with glory and honor...**"* (Heb 2:9)

Ruler/Subduer

- Adam: *"...replenish the earth, and **subdue it:** and **have dominion** over ...every living thing that moves upon the* *earth."* (Gen 1:28)

- Jesus: *"I have **conquered** the world." (John 16:33)*

Jesus was God's second Adam through which He has restored His likeness! More importantly is, unlike the first Adam, Jesus never relinquished that likeness. In Christ is God's True Opinion of humanity. I realized that I needed to adopt Jesus' understanding of this opinion. Consequently, if my self-awareness and self-perception are informed and formed by this true opinion, then I will have found my true identity, *who I am!*

In fact, the promise had been made known 2,000 years ago by Jesus himself, *"...as many as received Jesus, **God gave to them authority to be Sons of God** — to those trusting in His name, **who were born** not of blood, nor of will of flesh, nor of will of man, but **of God!**"* (John 1:12-13)

Notice, by believing that the Son of God had manifested in the flesh as Jesus the Son of Humanity, God would give me the authority to be a Son of God. This process is termed by God as a birth, but not of the flesh, but of the spirit – by God! The scripture sheds more light on this birth. The apostle Paul wrote, *"and because you are sons, **God sent forth the Spirit of His Son into our hearts**, crying out, '"Abba, Father!"'"* (Gal 4:6). Our acceptance of Jesus as the new Adam indicates that we too desire to be like him, Sons of God. God accomplishes our desire by giving us the *Life-Giving Spirit of His Son.* This results in our humanity being restored in the likeness of God. *The spirit of His Son remedies the corruptness of my spirit, that I too can be His Son!*

Here we have a New Creation process. In the beginning God first had formed humanity from the elements of the earth and the Spirit of Life. The result was humanity became a living being, which was in God's likeness, crowned with honor and glory, made a little lower than God.

Therefore, the process of the New Creation is similar. God sends forth into the believer the *Life-Giving Spirit of His Son*. Remember, Jesus is the Life, so in reality God sends forth the Spirit of Life into the heart of the believer. The result is the believer crying out *'Abba, Father!'* This indicates that the believer has received God's likeness, for the son is like the Father. In Christ – the new Adam, the believer has newly come forth from the hand of God, crowned with honor and glory and made a little lower than God. As the scripture affirms, *"Therefore if anyone is in Christ, **he is a new creation**..."* (2Cor 5:17).

In Christ, we are brought back to the Tree of Life as new creations. At the Tree of Life we are set free from the Curse of the Tree of the Knowledge of Good and Evil. Instead of inheritors of Death (separation from God), we now partake of Eternal Life with God. We are connected in our relationship with God, because we believe in His true opinion of us, which in turn informs and forms our self-awareness and self-perception, which in turn manifests into our reality.

What do I need to do to activate this new creation process? Receive Jesus, *the Son of your Humanity, as the Son of God*. This is so simple, yet so difficult for many, even Christians, to do. Many times I have heard it said, even by myself, *'There is more to it that just believe and receive! That is too simple!'* I now realize that was the mind of the Tree of the Knowledge of Good and Evil speaking. The mind of the Tree of Life says, *'Be it unto me as You have said!'*

CHAPTER 10
How I Received My True Identity

"...as many as received Jesus, **God gave to them authority to be Sons of God** *— to those trusting in His name,* **who were born** *not of blood, nor of will of flesh, nor of will of man, but* **of God!"** (John 1:12)

Notice, in this statement made by Jesus, two births are mentioned. There is a birth of blood, of the will of the flesh, of the will of man. This is the natural birth; this is the Adamic line of humanity being procreated from generation to generation.

The second birth however, is of the Spirit. Receiving Jesus results in the God-given authority (right, privilege and freedom) *to be born from above as Sons of God.* This is my True Identity. Here God undertakes to inform and form my identity – my awareness of what and who *I am.* This identity is now not informed by humanity's opinion of me, it is informed by God's opinion of me. He is the one who gives me the authority, the right, the privilege and freedom *to be his son.* Humanity may disagree, religion may condemn me, but God is the one that has given the authority, so I begin my journey into my True Identity without fear. For if God has given the authority, who can revoke it? Who can repeal that God-given right? Who can restrict that freedom? None other but myself. It is only I, like humanity in the garden, who can choose to reject that which God has given to me.

What does it mean to receive Jesus in this context? We know that Jesus identified as the Son of Humanity who was sent by God to be the Last Adam. I receive him as thus, as God's prototype of myself, a son of humanity. He is to be the hero, the role model, the goal, the aim and the aspiration of all humanity – in other words the new Father of Humanity.

That is how I see Jesus. I see him, as the Son of Humanity whose true identity was the divine Son of God. And as I see him thus, I am thus. I too am a son of humanity whose true identity is a divine Son of God. That identity has been given to me not by religion, nor earthly opinion, but by the authority of God.

» *That is how I see Jesus. I see him, as the Son of Humanity whose true identity was the divine Son of God. And as I see him thus, I am thus. I too am a son of humanity whose true identity is a divine Son of God.*

As an aside, if you are a female reading this book, you may wonder why the identity is of Son, and no mention of daughters. In the natural realm there are male and female genders. These genders are necessary for the procreation of life. However, in the spirit realm, God doesn't need a female to give birth to His sons, He simply does so by speaking forth the new life. Throughout the scriptures, the sons inherited all the possessions of the father. This was vividly portrayed in the case of Jesus being the Heir of His Father's Throne and Kingdom. Thus the identity of Son is closely tied to Christ himself. Since the birth of our new identity occurs in the spirit realm, the true Identity of Sons of God puts us in the position, like Christ, of inheriting everything from our Divine Father in the spirit realm. However, if you as a female are not comfortable identifying as a *'Son of God,'* maybe you could substitute the term *'Child of God'* just as well, for it is the quality of the identity that matters.

Returning to the topic at hand, I received Jesus by trusting that the Son of Humanity's true identity was that of Divine Son of God. I have received him by understanding that I too am a son of humanity whose true identity is a Divine Son of God. My self-awareness and self-perception are to be informed by this truth, and will result in God forming my identity, and bringing it to pass by His divine power. I am born as that which I received, not of blood, nor of will of flesh, nor of will of man, but of God! It seems too good to be true!

But why should it seem too good to be true? It is because fallen humanity is still accustomed to eating from the Tree of the Knowledge of Good and Evil. Humanity has been trained to believe nothing is free, especially from God. We have been trained (especially by religion) that the things of God are far away out of our reach. We are accustomed to *'working our way'* to heaven, with the inevitable results being *'thorns and thistles.'* The nagging thought in the back of our minds remains that we had better not offend our bipolar Father, lest *"he break out" against us...* (Exod 19:24). These are all opinions in harmony with the Tree of the Knowledge of Good and Evil. The Son of God came with the message of the Tree of Life. He said, *"Come to me, all you who labor and are loaded down, and I will give you rest."* (Matt 11:28)

The distorted opinions of humanity and the paradigm of the Tree of the Knowledge of Good and Evil, load us down with religious burdens, which we bear unnecessarily. They foster in us unhealthy self-perceptions that God never intended for us. Jesus gives us the true words of Life that free us from these faith-sapping beliefs.

The apostle Paul wrote, *"For you did not receive the spirit of slavery to fall back into fear, but you have received **the Spirit of adoption as sons**, by which we cry, 'Abba! Father!'"* (Rom 8:15). Receiving the Son of Humanity as your own humanity, leads us to be given the Spirit, which gives us his divinity as Sons of God. A new creation is manifested. We are then brought back to the Tree of Life. We can truly cry out to our Heavenly Father – *"Daddy!"* No longer do we relate to God as a slave to a master, but as a son to his father. No longer do we receive an evil wage, but a glorious permanent inheritance. No longer death (eternal separation from God) and condemnation, but eternal life and affirmation. The Lord promised, *"So you are **no longer a slave, but a Son**, and if a Son, then **an Heir** through God."* (Gal 4:7)

I have received my true identity. *This is who **I am**!* Not according to parents, friends, enemies, society, religion or circumstances, but according to God. This is God's opinion of me. I choose to believe what God has said and I know that He in turn will work in me, for me and through me to bring to pass all things associated with my true identity.

By receiving my true identity, I have been resurrected from the death of Adam. The spirit-inspired apostle wrote, *"For as indeed **in Adam all are dying**, so also **in Christ all will be made alive...**"* (1Cor 15:22). The death of Adam was through the corruption of the likeness of God, which resulted in him separating himself and his posterity from God. That death had been passed on to all humanity. The corruption of the glorious identity caused humanity to continuously reject life, choosing religion instead. However, as 4,000 years have proven, *"...if a law had been given that was able to make us alive, then truly righteousness would have been by Law..."* (Gal 3:21). The way of the Tree of the Knowledge of Good and Evil had to be allowed to play out its bitter wages – frustration, condemnation, failure and death.

As humanity sought to climb up the ladder to heaven, the Law accused them day and night of missing the mark. God had told Moses, *"Take this book of the Law, and put it in the side of the ark of the covenant of Jehovah your God, **that it may be there for a witness against you...**"* (Deut 31:26). The Law witnessed against humanity's attempts to be accepted by God via obedience to lists of moral Do's and Don'ts. The Law witnessed against humanity's ignorance of God's opinion of them. The Law witnessed against humanity's unbelief – their distrust of God's Character, Power and Promises. The Law enforced punishments, which portrayed the eternal consequences of the way of the Tree of the Knowledge of Good and Evil.

> » *When I receive my identity from God, I am instantly resurrected – Raised to Life from the death curse, which was from the Tree of the Knowledge of Good and Evil!*

However, in Christ, I am rescued from that death, from humanity's separation from God, which Adam had chosen. That deliverance from death is a *'raising up,'* or resurrection to life. It is written, *"But God, being rich in mercy, because of the great love with which he loved us, even **when we were dead in our failures, made us alive together with Christ** – by grace you have been saved – and **raised us up with him** and seated us with him in the heavenly places in Christ Jesus!"* (Eph 2:4-6). This is truly wonderful! The paradigm of the Tree of the Knowledge of Good and Evil had us in consistent failure, missing the mark of the glory of God. Now in Christ, the likeness of God has been restored, resulting in a resurrection to life. God has resurrected me together with Christ and raised me to sit with him in the heavenly spirit realm! The Spirit of Life has brought me into the presence of God before the Tree of Life. Wow! There is so much that I need to learn about living in this realm. However, I am confident that I have the rest of eternity to grow in knowledge and favor as I enjoy this eternal life.

CHAPTER 11
Faith Wins; Unbelief Loses

Faith is essential for receiving and living the identity of Sons of God. Faith is one of those words that seems to be very difficult to grasp. It is definitely not a rare or unknown word, especially in the Christian religion. Within the King James Version of the Bible, the word faith occurs over 200 times. So it is not a word that is unheard of, but it might as well be, since the lack of faith has been humanity's ruin from the beginning.

In the context of this book, the essence of faith is the exercise and possession of trust and confidence toward God's Character, Ability and Promises.

God's Character:

- Life, Love, Faithful, Trustworthy, Righteous, Fair, Generous, Gracious, Tenderhearted, Abundant in good things, etc.

God's Ability:

- All powerful; all possible; will never forsake; defeats enemies; changes the heart of humanity; removes consequences of missing the mark; causes even the negative and unpleasant circumstances to turn out for our benefit; provides for all needs and aspirations; gives life; heals and restores; giver of good gifts, etc.

God's Promises:

- The adoption and new birth as Sons of God. The divine inheritance. The Kingdom of Heaven. Reigning with

Christ. Ask and it shall be given to you. Believe and you shall receive... etc.

Unbelief is a type of faith, but it is not based on God's Character, Ability and Promises. Unbelief is the exercise and possession of trust and confidence in humanity's ability and knowledge. Thus true Faith springs from the Tree of Life, while Unbelief springs from the Tree of the Knowledge of Good and Evil.

Therefore, we can see that the identity of Sons of God comes from the Tree of Life. If we are seeking our identity according to the paradigm of the Tree of the Knowledge of Good and Evil, we would not be able to receive the identity of Sons of God. The Tree of the Knowledge of Good and Evil focuses on humanity's ability and knowledge. The identity of Sons of God focuses on God's Character, Ability and Promises. In order to prosper in this identity, every opinion concerning what and who we are, must be based on God's Character, Ability and Promises. The Bible narrative portrays examples of Faith versus Unbelief. I have chosen two examples of how humanity chose to exercise Faith and Unbelief, and what were the results of those respective choices.

Abraham and Sarah's Faith

Abraham is termed *'the Father of those who have faith,'* because God had commended him on his faith. However, Abraham had to go through a lengthy process, moving him from unbelief to faith. That process took over twenty years. God had promised Abraham that he and his wife Sarah would have a child. According to the narrative, at that time Sarah was infertile – she could not conceive children. Abraham and Sarah first chose to exercise unbelief toward God's promise. Remember, Unbelief is the exercise and possession of trust and confidence in humanity's ability and knowledge. So Abraham decided to conceive the child with Sarah's Egyptian slave-girl Hagar. By doing this he was trusting in what he could do, instead of trusting in what *God had promised to do, in His Faithfulness to them and in His ability to make it happen.* The child that was born to Abraham and Hagar was Ishmael. Abraham and Sarah rejoiced over Ishmael, because they thought that he was the fulfillment of God's promise.

Several years after the birth of Ishmael, however, God revealed to Abraham that His promise still stood – that Abraham would indeed have a child, not with a slave-girl, but with his wife Sarah. Both Abraham and Sarah were incredulous because by that time, Sarah had passed the age of child-bearing, so even if she had been healthy, she still would not have been able to get pregnant. Abraham, at the age of 100 years-old, according to the scriptures had become *'dead'* (Rom 4:19), which is a politically correct way of saying that he had become sexually impotent. However, God had insisted that it would happen, assuring them, *"Is any thing too hard for the LORD?"* (Gen 18:14)

» *The focus of faith is not on the impossibility of the situation, but on the promise of God, and His faithfulness and ability to keep that promise.*

At that time, it was past Abraham and Sarah's ability and knowledge to produce this child. They were both forced, because of the impossibility of the circumstances, to trust in God's Character, Ability and Promises – to exercise complete Faith in Him. When they had done that, God revived Abraham's virility and restored Sarah's womb. She was able to conceive and bear the promised child, Isaac.

According to the apostle Paul, Abraham *"**considered his body already having become dead**, being about a hundred years old, **and the lifelessness of Sarah's womb**."*

"Yet he did not waver through unbelief at the promise of God, but was strengthened in faith, having given glory to God, and having been fully assured that what God had promised, He is also able to do." (Rom 4:19-21). Notice how Abraham, having considered the impossibility of humanity's ability and knowledge to change the circumstances of his one-hundred-year-old body and the deadness of his wife's womb, decided to choose Faith instead of Unbelief. Notice how his Faith was informed by the promise of God and the Ability of God, and as such his Faith was rewarded.

In the case of Sarah, it was revealed, *"By faith also Sarah, herself barren, received power for the conception of seed, even beyond the opportune age, since she considered the One having promised, to be faithful..."* (Heb 11:11). Notice that God's Character of Faithfulness informed Sarah's Faith, and as such her Faith was rewarded.

Thus we see that the example of Rewarding Faith is of one that is formed and informed by God's Character, Ability and Promises. The focus of faith is not on the impossibility of the situation, but on the promise of God, and His faithfulness and ability to keep that promise. This focus is vital in receiving fully our new identity.

Israel's Unbelief in the Wilderness

The Bible narrative also gives one of the most tragic examples of Unbelief. This experience occurred during Israel's journey from Egypt to Canaan.

As He had done for Abraham, God made promises to Israel. At the time, Israel was in a predicament of impossible circumstances. They had been enslaved in Egypt for 400 years. For a while their lives were initially not overburdened. Even though their social status was that of slaves, there was still a measure of restraint toward them by the Egyptians in honor of their ancestor Joseph, who had been instrumental in advising Egypt on how to survive a seven-year famine. Even as slaves, the Israelites lived relatively comfortably, being beneficiaries of Egypt's prosperity.

However, after four centuries had passed, the fame of Joseph had been forgotten, and the Egyptians began to despise their Israelite slaves. The Egyptian king passed harsh laws that seemed intent upon their extermination. So the Israelite people cried out in distress and God intervened. He chose Moses, an Israelite who had been raised in the Pharaoh's household, to be the instrument of their deliverance out of Egypt, into a land He had prepared for them. At that time, God promised Israel that He would certainly deliver them out of the hand of the Pharaoh, despite the king's opposition to them.

According to the Bible narrative, God told Israel, *"I will bring you out from under the burdens of the Egyptians, and I will rid you out of their bondage, and I will redeem you with a stretched out arm, and with great judgments: And I will take you to me for a people, and I will be to you a God: and all of you shall know that I am Yahweh your God, which brings you out from under the burdens of the Egyptians. And I will bring you in unto the land, concerning the which I did swear to give it to Abraham, to Isaac, and to Jacob; and I will give it you for an heritage..."* (Exod 6:6-8)

God reassured Moses that even though the Pharaoh was unwilling to free the Israelites, He would ensure that they would be freed. *"I am sure that the king of Egypt will not let you go, no, not by a mighty hand. And I will stretch out my hand, and strike*

*Egypt with all my wonders which I will do in the midst thereof: and after that **he will let you go.***" (Exod 3:19-20). Thus we see that God expressed His desire to save, not destroy, Israel. He promised to deliver them, not kill them. He indicated that He was already prepared for the pharaoh's obstinate heart. However, as the narrative progressed, we see that it seemed impossible for Israel to take God at His word. Their continued perspective of God was one of distrust. They seemed incapable of Faith. Instead, they manifested persistent Unbelief.

At every point of perceived difficulty, instead of seeking God's assistance and trusting in His promise, they instead cried out against Him. After God had succeeded in breaking the will of the Egyptians by allowing them to be ravaged with deadly plagues, the Israelites were finally let go. As they journeyed out of Egypt they came to the Red Sea, which was in the way. By this time, the Egyptians had overcome their initial terror and they had decided to eliminate all the freed Israelites. The pharaoh gathered his army and led them after the people, and came upon them at the shore of the Red Sea.

When the Israelites saw the armies of Egypt in the distance, they immediately voiced their Unbelief. They cried unto Moses, *"Because there were no graves in Egypt, **have you taken us away to die in the wilderness?** Wherefore have you dealt thus with us, to carry us forth out of Egypt? Is not this the word that we did tell you in Egypt, saying, 'Let us alone, that we may serve the Egyptians?' **For it had been better for us to serve the Egyptians, than that we should die in the wilderness!**"* (Exod 14:11-12)

These accusations indicate that the Israelites had never believed the promises of God. Because of this, they would always voice their true feelings in times of difficulty. Here they accused Moses of bringing them out of Egypt to die in the wilderness. Their accusations against Moses were in truth condemnations against God, for Moses was His prophet. They had no confidence in God's Character, Ability and Promises. Instead, they looked to their own limited knowledge and ability.

Even though God had manifested great patience with them, still delivering them out of every difficulty, they still refused to renew their opinion of Him. Their final straw came, when they had come to the border of the promised land. Having sent spies into the land, the report came back that giants inhabited the country, and that it was impossible for them to take possession of it. Once more, they failed to trust God, even though by that time, they had experienced ample evidence of His Character, Ability and Promises by the way He had delivered them out of every previous impossible situation. They chose, as usual, to ignore these plain proofs and instead continued to accuse God again of being intent on their destruction. According to the narrative, Israel wept, "... *wherefore has the LORD brought us unto this land,* ***to fall by the sword, that our wives and our children should be a prey?*** *Were it not better for us to return into Egypt?"* (Num 14:3)

» *By failing to manifest Faith, even with their experiences of all the past times of deliverance, Israel finally had condemned themselves. They became victims of their own words. Jesus had said, "For with that verdict you pronounce, you will be judged; and with that measure you measure, it will be measured to you."*

By failing to manifest Faith, even with their experiences of all the past times of deliverance, Israel finally had condemned themselves. They became victims of their own words. Jesus had said, *"For* ***with that verdict you pronounce, you will be judged;*** *and with that measure you measure, it will be measured to you,"* (Matt 7:2) and so it was with Israel. Israel judged God to be untrustworthy, unfaithful, uncaring and unable to deliver them. They fully manifested the mindset of the Tree of the Knowledge of Good and Evil. Their unjust judgment of God's motives came back upon them, they were shown to be not worthy of trust, unbelieving, not worthy of being cared for, nor delivered, based on their unbelieving opinion of God. God therefore said; *"what you have said in my hearing will be done to you: your dead bodies shall fall in this wilderness, and of all your number ...who have grumbled against me, not one shall come into the land where I swore that I would make you dwell, **except Caleb the son of Jephunneh and Joshua the son of Nun**."* (Num 14:28-30). Just as they had insisted that God was intent on their destruction, their own opinion of God was allowed to become their reality!

Out of the entire number of Israelite adults, only Caleb and Joshua were spared. The rest of that generation of Israel died in the wilderness during a period of forty years. Only Caleb and Joshua remained of that first generation. Why was Caleb and Joshua spared of that judgment? It was because they were the only ones who had expressed Faith in God's Character, Ability and Promises. They had exhorted Israel to Faith instead of Unbelief. According to the narrative, they had said, *"The land, ... is an exceedingly good land. If the LORD delights in us, **he will bring us into this land and give it to us**, a land that flows with milk and honey. ...And **do not fear the people of the land, ... Their protection is removed from them**, and the LORD is with us..."* (Num 14:7-9)

Caleb and Joshua believed in God's Character, Ability and Promises. They saw that He was good, and that He loved Israel and desired only good for them. They believed that what He had promised, He was more than able to accomplish. *Their Faith saved them!* But Israel's persistent refusal to trust God, essentially tied His hands from acting in their favor and on their behalf.

Thus, instead of God's desire being fulfilled for them, their own distorted opinion of God became a self-fulfilling destruction to them.

Object Lessons for us today

These experiences of the ancient people's Faith and Unbelief are object lessons for us today in the context of our identity. Our true identity is based on God's opinion of us. It is therefore of utmost importance that we ascertain what is God's true opinion of us! In my opinion, many Christians still have not been informed of God's true opinion. Many are like the Israelites in the wilderness, manifesting tragic unbelief toward God. Some also seem not able to accept God's true opinion of them. Instead they prefer to manifest what they believe is *'humility and reverent fear,'* not wanting to confess their true identity, feeling that it would be tantamount to blasphemy. If we do not trust God's opinion, we cannot receive that identity. Thus like ancient Israel, they wander around in the wilderness of unbelief, never receiving God's wonderful opinion.

Or maybe, like Abraham's begetting of Ishmael, we may attempt to make ourselves into Sons of God. Many believe that they must do some great works, and be perfect in their list-keeping, in order to *'attain'* to the identity. This also is Unbelief, for it is based on humanity's knowledge and ability. Our natural birth into the flesh was not based on anything we did; it was based on what our parents did. Likewise, our spiritual birth is not based on anything we do, but on what our Heavenly Father has done. The only thing that is necessary for God to manifest that new birth, is our faith in His ability to bring us into that reality.

This chapter has given examples of how humanity views God's

opinion of them. In the next chapter, I will look at humanity's view of God Himself.

CHAPTER 12
Two Reports about God, Contrasted

We have learned that there are two reports about God's Opinion of humanity – a distorted one and a True one. These reports are concerning God's feelings toward humanity - How He views us. In this chapter, I wish to delve in a little more into a related aspect of these reports, which is, what kind of person is God? This aspect is concerning God's character. There are two reports about the quality of God's Character. The distorted one also is from the Tree of the Knowledge of Good and Evil, and the true one from the Tree of Life. The distorted report was concocted from the lips of the evil one. That false report hides the true God from humanity. As it were, it closes humanity's eyes while claiming to open them.

Jesus, who had the true report from the Tree of Life, said, *"no one knows who the Son is except the Father, or who the Father is except the Son and anyone to whom the Son chooses to reveal him."* (Luke 10:22). This is extremely important for us to remember, the revelation of God's true character as presented in the old scriptures is not easily discernible. Only through Jesus' revelation of His Father can the truth of God and His Sons be seen. God's glory as revealed through Moses was only his *'hind parts,' but not his face*. The face displays a person's true identity and character. We identify persons by their faces. We see their emotions through their faces. We can see tenderness in their eyes, even though their actions might be saying otherwise. This is exactly what has happened under the paradigm of the Tree of the Knowledge of Good and Evil. God's face had been hidden, not because He desired it to be hidden, but because humanity had been convinced that God is hideous.

The apostle wrote, *"...their minds were hardened; for until the*

*present day, the same veil remains at the reading of the old cov-
enant, not being lifted, which is being removed in Christ. But
unto this day, when Moses shall be read, **a veil lies over their
heart**. But **whenever one shall have turned to the Lord, the veil
is taken away**...*" (2Cor 3:14-16). The distorted report about
God has hardened humanity's mind. It is nigh impossible for humanity to see the True character of God, especially in the traditional reading of the Old Covenant. That covenant ministered the
death and harshness chosen by humanity when they ate from the
Tree of the Knowledge of Good and Evil. The old covenant did
not fully represent God's true opinion of humanity. It however,
reflected humanity's flawed opinion of God. That is why it cannot remove the veil that hides the face of God. This veil is over
humanity's hardened heart, masking God's face! The problem
lies in humanity's opinion of God, not God's opinion of humanity! Only when a person accepts the Truth about God's Opinion
of humanity, does that veil remove. When that veil is removed,
we see God with new eyes; in fact our eyes are truly opened.
Our relationship to Him undergoes a drastic change, from that
of a Slave-to-Master to that of a Son-to-Father. It is only when
we receive the truth as it is in Jesus, that we can see the face of
God – His True feelings about us.

Remember at the giving of the old covenant, the people were
once again terrified of God. They cried out, *"let not God speak
with us, lest we die!"* (Exod 20:19). Like their ancestors, they
feared that God desired to destroy their lives. They begged God
to cease speaking to them! But we must always remember, that
God's true feelings about humanity were not reflected within the
old scriptures. God was simply honoring the paradigm that humanity had chosen in the Garden. Moses partly understood this.
He said to Israel, ***"Do not fear**, for God has come to test you,
that the fear of him may be before you, that you may not sin..."*
(Exod 20:20). Notice Moses pleaded for them not to be afraid

of God. However, *the Lord was using fear to motivate them to not sin!* Understand the difference. The fear was to motivate the people to obey the Law, but God Himself desired Love, not fear. Thus was the conflict between the paradigm of the Tree of the Knowledge of Good and Evil, and the Tree of Life. Because of the Tree of the Knowledge of Good and Evil, fear had come in and God used fear to motivate. However, in reality, if humanity could really see the truth about God, they would realize that He is not to be feared. He is not a terrifying offended tyrant, but a humble and kind-hearted Father.

Jesus declared that, *"**no one has ever yet seen God**. The only begotten Son, the one being in the bosom of the Father, he has made Him known..."* (John 1:18). This is why God had commanded that we listen to His Son. The previous revelations of God in the ancient scriptures need to be reviewed through what has been revealed of the Father by His Son. This is why Jesus declared, *"If you had known me, you would also have known my Father. **From now you know Him, and have seen Him**."* (John 14:7). Jesus let us know that he was the true image – the visible representation – of His invisible Father.

If humanity wants to know what God is like, look at Jesus. If we want to know how God feels about humanity, discern how Jesus felt about humanity. The previous revelations through the prophets were given under the shadow of the Tree of the Knowledge of Good and Evil. That is why Jesus claimed, *"...no one has gone up into heaven except the one having come down out of heaven, the Son of Man..."* (John 3:13). The revelation of God from Jesus superseded all previous revelations that had been given. The revelation that Jesus brought was a *living revelation,* embodied in himself. Jesus contrasted the previous revelations concerning God in very extreme ways. In John's gospel, Jesus is recorded as saying, *"All who ever came before me are thieves and robbers...*" (John 10:8). In comparison to the revelation of the Father that the Son gave, the limited revelations of God in the old scriptures, which came before the advent of Jesus, were as the day compared to the night. When we begin to see God from Jesus' perspective, we are able to see the Father behind the blood-soaked mask, which He wore in the old scriptures. That mask was humanity's corrupted opinion of God.

Is the Lord 'a Hard Man?'

Jesus told a parable about a servant, whose master gave him a sum of money to invest for a fixed period of time. At the end of the period, the master returned to inquire of the performance of the servant's investment.

The servant however, had chosen not to invest the funds, and when the master came, he returned the exact sum of money to his employer. The servant said to the master, *"Master, **I knew you to be a hard man**, reaping where you did not sow, and gathering where you scattered no seed, so I was afraid, and I went and hid your talent in the ground. Here you have what is yours."* (Matthew 25:24-25). The talent was a form of ancient currency. In today's money, the value of a talent would be around one and a half million US dollars.

Since this is a parable, we know that the individuals are symbolic. The master represented God, while this servant represented a class of humanity. This parable reveals how humanity views God, versus what God really is like. Humanity's view has largely been informed by the report about God that has been believed under the paradigm of the Tree of the Knowledge of Good and Evil.

Let's see the characteristics that the servant attributed to his master.

- You are a hard man

- You reap where you did not sow

- You gather where you did not scatter

- I am afraid of you

We can see clearly that this view of God echoes the sentiments of Adam and Eve under the spell of the adversary's lies. Many persons today have a similar evil view of God, not realizing that they have been deceived by a false report about Him.

The servant had said, *"Master, **I knew you to be a hard man**..."* Under the paradigm of the Tree of the Knowledge of Good and Evil, God was presented as harsh, unreasonable, unfair, uncaring and demanding, not gentle and kind. This is as a result of humanity's distorted view of God's opinion of them. This is why the Old Testament scriptures seemed to depict Him as being savage, bloodthirsty and altogether violent. This was partly due to the perception of humanity being informed by a false report about God and partly due to the ministration of death. We remember that God had warned humanity that if they chose the Tree of the Knowledge of Good and Evil, the consequence would be death. As a result of their belief that they needed to labour tirelessly to be accepted by a perfectionist God, He was presented to humanity as being an evil tyrant under that paradigm. The bad stuff that happened to them was attributed to God. They failed to understand that their predicament came about as the consequences of their own actions.

> » *Under the paradigm of the Tree of the Knowledge of Good and Evil, God was presented as harsh, unreasonable, unfair, uncaring and demanding, not gentle and kind. This is as a result of humanity's distorted view of God's opinion of them. This is why the Old Testament scriptures seemed to depict Him as being savage, bloodthirsty and altogether violent.*

However, even under such an unfair report about Himself, God's true character still shone through. We remember God's abundant kindness to Israel. Yet on multiple occasions they still held on to their fear that He had intended to kill them all. Because of the overwhelming spell of the evil report and paradigm, they could not see His goodness and love. Thus while they were quite willing to be His servants and keep all the lists of Do's and Don'ts, *they could not bring themselves to trust Him nor love Him.*

But is God truly *'a hard man?'* Jesus demonstrated that God is a tender and kindhearted Father. According to the apostle James, *"...the Lord is large-hearted and compassionate..."* (Jas 5:11). In the parable, the master had given the servant *a free gift of enormous value!* Yet the servant accused the master of *'reaping where he did not sow.'* But the truth was that the master had indeed sowed to the servant one talent, the equivalent of one and a half million US dollars! Thus we see that this servant had a veil over his heart – his mind, which caused him to see his master as evil, when the truth was otherwise.

According to the parable, the servant was judged according to his own distorted belief! The master enquired of him, *"**You knew that I reap where I have not sown and gather where I scattered no seed? Then you ought to have invested my money with the bankers...**"* (Matt 25:26-27). Many who preach the 'gospel' of an exacting God, fail to realize that they are actually condemning themselves, for they themselves do not measure up to the requirements of the very gospel they preach! This servant's 'gospel' was that his master was harsh, unreasonable, unfair, uncaring and demanding. This very 'gospel' so filled him with dread, that he was paralyzed with fear of maybe making a wrong investment, so instead he did nothing with the money entrusted to him. Thus his own distorted view of his master was his own destruction.

The servant was dismissed, they *"cast out the worthless servant, into the **outer darkness**, where there will be weeping and **gnashing of teeth**..."* (Matt 25:30). The darkness symbolized ignorance. This ignorance would be in reality the ignored evidence of God's True Character. The apostle John is adamant, *"God is Love!"* (1John 4:8), and again, *"God is Light, and in Him is no darkness at all!"* (1John 1:5). I know Christians who are vehemently opposed to the idea that God loves everyone unconditionally. Some still hold on to the old mask, which God had worn under the paradigm of the Tree of the Knowledge of Good and Evil, insisting that He is *"a jealous God..."* (Exod 20:5). Jesus came to reveal that the Truth was, *"Love is patient, is kind. **Love is not jealous**..."* (1Cor 13:4).

Many are still in darkness, with the veil still on their hardened hearts. The condition of *'gnashing of teeth'* was based on a Hebrew idiom, which described the action of a person who is accusing, full of fury and indignation against someone. For example, the accusers of Stephen *"began gnashing the teeth at him."* (Acts 7:54). Many people gnash their teeth at God when Christians zealously attribute to God the violent storms and killer earthquakes – *'acts of God.'* They see Him according to the old paradigm, a destroyer and killer. However, Jesus revealed that *"**the Thief** is not coming except that **he should be stealing and sacrificing and destroying. I came that they may have life*** *eternal, and have it superabundantly..."* (John 10:10). Notice, Jesus associated the report of a violent God with the *'Thief'* – the robber who had instigated that evil report in the Garden at the Tree of the Knowledge of Good and Evil. He however associated himself and his Father with the Tree of Super-abundant Life.

Many gnash their teeth at other Christians who choose to relate to God as a loving Father instead of an exacting Master. Thus we see that the end result of the distorted report is that it causes humanity to be angry with God and His Sons. In apostolic times, this played out in the horrendous persecution of the early Christians by the Jews. The Jews refused to accept the report concerning God that Jesus and his early church gave. Instead they steadfastly held on to the old report. That report keeps many in a perpetual state of terror of God. They believe that God is *'a hard man'* and in turn they enforce the harsh rigor of religious burdens on others *in the name of God*.

Many Christians are still trembling in dread at the thought of a terrible God. While they themselves would never wish their own children to be terrified of them, they somehow hold on to the notion that our Father wishes us to *'fear Him'* and to *'tremble before Him.'* These are attributes of God that were perpetuated by the paradigm of the Tree of the Knowledge of Good and Evil. God's children do not relate to Him on the basis of fear, but on love. We come to Him as our large-hearted and compassionate Father.

As part of the renewing of our mind, we need to examine every opinion we have of our heavenly Father, to see if it is really *the Truth as presented by Jesus*. Every opinion we have of God, which has the shadow of the Tree of the Knowledge of Good and Evil over it, will result in an irrational distrust of God, and an equivalent tyrannical attitude toward our brethren.

CHAPTER 13
How to Confess Christ and Deny the Flesh

Thus far we have seen that there are two ways that humanity relates to God. Those two ways are based on whether humanity chooses to exercise Faith or Unbelief in God's true opinion of humanity. The way of Faith is of the Tree of Life, while the way of Unbelief is of the Tree of the Knowledge of Good and Evil.

As I have shown thus far, the way of the Tree of the Knowledge of Good and Evil puts one under a system of performance. It is a system of moral Do's and Don'ts, the goal of which is to become like God. However, when we consider this closely, there is obviously nothing that fallen humanity can do to become like God. Thus humanity's quest to become like God is bound to be a futile one. It is like climbing a ladder from earth to heaven, where each slip causes the climber to start again from the first rung. Such a quest cannot change humanity into divinity, for as Jesus said, *"that having been born of the flesh is flesh, and that having been born of the Spirit is spirit..."* (John 3:6). Flesh begets flesh and spirit begets spirit. One cannot beget the other.

Fallen humanity are all the descendants of the first Adam, and as such are inheritors of a likeness that is corrupted. This corrupted likeness is called the 'Flesh' and encapsulates all that humanity is when it is devoid of the Divine Nature. That which is born of the Flesh is Flesh. Flesh can only produce, or give birth to, Flesh. Since God is Spirit and Divine, the only way to be like God is to be born of the Spirit of God, or as Jesus put it, *"It is necessary for you all to be born from above..."* (John 3:7). This new birth is initiated by choosing to have Faith in God's Truth concerning your identity. The Truth is likened to a seed, or sperm, which is received into the womb of the mind, and then conceives a new life that is of the Spirit, like God, who is also Spirit. This new life is generated under the lineage of the Last Adam, or Christ. The scripture declares, *"And because you are sons,* **God sent forth the Spirit of His Son into your hearts***, crying, 'Abba, Father!'"* (Gal 4:6)

When I am born of the Spirit, my spirit is connected to God's Spirit in a new relation, that of a Father and Son. I am counseled to confess my new Father-Son relationship, and deny my old Master-Slave relationship. Also I have been transferred from the lineage of Adam, to the lineage of God. My Spirit lineage is that which is eternal, while my Adamic lineage was temporal. In other words, the *'Me'* identity is of the Spirit. The Adamic body of flesh that was prepared for *'Me'* was from the elements of the ground, and will return there one day. However the *'Me'* is Spirit and returns to my Father who is also Spirit. After the death of the body, I cannot continue unto God if I hadn't received God's opinion. This is not because God rejects me, but because I would reject God. Just like Adam and Eve sought to hide from God's presence because of their fear and torment, an unconverted spirit would experience extreme torment since it had not received the Truth about God's opinion. Think about it, if a person had not received the Truth that God loves them unconditionally, then that person would be terrified to come into the presence of God, and would be destroyed by that fear. Adam and Eve experienced this severe dread in the Garden after they chose to believe the serpent and ate of the Tree of the Knowledge of Good and Evil. Their 'eyes' – their self-perception and self-awareness – were changed. Instead of experiencing fullness of joy and eternal pleasures in God's presence, they experienced extreme terror.

Adam told God, *"I heard your voice in the garden, and* **I was afraid***, because I was naked; and* **I hid myself***..."* (Gen 3:10).

God's presence, which before had wrought in them favorable emotions of Joy and Pleasure, was now met with Fear and Shame. Terrified humanity hid from God. What changed? Did God change? Moreover, did God's opinion of humanity change? Or was it that humanity's opinion of God had changed? I believe it was the latter. Humanity's opinion of God had changed. Why did humanity's opinion of God change? It changed because *humanity believed that God had changed His opinion of them.* Thus they were now relating to God based on a false narrative that had been fed to them by the serpent. That narrative was essentially: *'God knows you are not like Him, God is not pleased with you and you have to try very hard to please God and to be like Him.'*

» *Why did humanity's opinion of God change? It changed because humanity believed that God had changed His opinion of them. Thus they were now relating to God based on a false narrative that had been fed to them by the serpent.*

This false narrative caused them to perceive themselves accordingly. *'We are not like God, thus we need to hide from him. God is not pleased with us thus need to be terrified of Him. We need to please God by our perfect performance; otherwise we will be cast out of His presence.'* However, the reason why humanity was removed from the presence of God and the Tree of Life was not because God had changed His opinion of them, it was because they could no longer stand to be in His presence! They no longer trusted Him and they were terrified that He would harm them! God in His mercy could not allow them to live eternally in that wretched state.

However, we can thank God that through the work that He has done by Christ on humanity's behalf, we can now be brought back to the choice that Adam originally had – to choose from the

Tree of Life or from the Tree of the Knowledge of Good and Evil.
We can choose to believe the opinion of God concerning humanity, and reject the opinion of the Enemy. This is called *'Confessing Christ and Denying the Flesh.'* In *'Confessing Christ and
Denying the Flesh,'* the Likeness of God is formed in us, and our
Spirit identity grows and strengthens. We are no longer terrified
of God and we are assured of his love for us, and his acceptance
of us. Let us look at what *'Confessing Christ and Denying the
Flesh'* means in practical terms.

My Lineage – In Adam versus In Christ

As someone who has been born of the Spirit, I have been given a
new lineage. The scripture speaks of two lineages – that of Adam
and that of Christ (the Last Adam). My First Birth was in the lineage of fallen Adam, and is referred to as being born of the flesh.
When I accepted God's True opinion of me however, I was born
of the Spirit, in the lineage of Christ. The lineage of Christ is
vastly superior over the lineage of Adam. Jesus said, *"that having been born of the flesh is flesh, and that having been born of
the Spirit is spirit..."* (John 3:6). Humanity born in the lineage
of Adam was permanently under the condemnation of the Law as
they attempted Godlikeness via the performance of lists of moral
Do's and Don'ts. The apostle Paul referred to that method as the
"...righteousness which is of the Law..." (Phil 3:9). However,
Jesus possessed the Righteousness of God, which is flawless,
therefore the Law could not find fault with him. When we are
born of the spirit we have been placed in that faultless lineage
of Christ. In that righteous lineage, the Law cannot condemn us.
The good news proclaims, *"therefore there is now **no condemnation to those in Christ Jesus."*** (Rom 8:1). For simplicity sake
I will contrast these two lineages in table form, that the characteristics of each can be easily grasped.

LINEAGE IN ADAM	LINEAGE IN CHRIST (Last Adam)
Born Sinner (Rom 5:19)	**Born** *Again* **Righteous** (Rom 5:19; Eph 4:24)
Unrighteous (Rom 3:10)	**God's Righteous Nature** (Phil 3:9; 2 Peter 1:4; Rom 3:21-22)
Ruled by Sin and Death (Rom 5:12)	**Ruled by Righteousness and Life** (Rom 5:17; 2 Cor 5:21)
Flesh (Romans 7:5; John 3:6)	**Spirit** (Romans 8:9; John 3:6)
Living Soul (1Cor 15:45)	**Life-giving Spirit** (1Cor 15:45)
Natural (1Cor 15:46)	**Spiritual** (1Cor 15:46)
Earthy (1Cor 15:48)	**Heavenly** (1Cor 15:48)
Corrupt (1Cor 15:50)	**Incorrupt** (1Pet 1:23)

Notice that the characteristics of the Adamic-Lineage are completely unlike those of the Christ-Lineage. However, most worthy of note is that the two Lineages operate on the Law of Heredity. In other words, I did nothing to become a sinner in the Adamic-Lineage, I simply inherited that characteristic as part of that lineage when I was born. As we may say, *'I was born that way.'*

Likewise, I did nothing to become perfectly righteous when I was born again, since the righteousness of God is inherent with the Christ-Lineage, *I simply inherited that characteristic as part of that nature when I was born again from above.* We may as well say, *'I was **born again** that way.'* The referenced scripture affirms that I am *"found in [Christ], not having a righteousness of my own that comes from the law [a list of moral Do's and Don'ts], but that which comes through faith in Christ, **the righteousness from God** that depends on Faith!"* (Phil 3:9)

The characteristics listed in the table are not all, but I encourage you to peruse the scriptures to see if you discover more. However, let me give a practical example of *'Confessing Christ and Denying the Flesh'* using this table. Let's use the Adamic-Lineage's characteristics of Sin and Death (Rom 5:12) and the Christ-Lineage's Righteousness and Life (Rom 5:17). According to the scripture reference, *"just as sin entered into the world through one man, and death through sin, so **also death passed to all men, because all sinned."** (Rom 5:12) Here we see that the one man – Adam – missed the mark and as a result death (or eternal separation from life) came into the world, and all humanity inherited this Adamic-Lineage of death, constantly missing the mark.

The contrasting lineage – the Christ-Lineage – is spoken of in the other scripture reference, *"For if, by the trespass of the one [Adam], death reigned through the one [Adam], how much more will **those receiving the abundance of loving-kindness and of the gift of righteousness, reign in life through the one – Jesus Christ!"** (Rom 5:17). In this lineage, instead of the characteristic of death and sin, the Christ-Lineage has the inherited characteristic of righteousness and life, which are actually characteristics of God, our Father.

In *'Confessing Christ and Denying the Flesh,'* we confess the characteristics of the Christ-Lineage as being true concerning ourselves, while denying and rejecting the characteristics of the Adamic-Lineage. So for instance, I may confess, *"In Christ I am fully alive and perfectly righteous!"* As well I may proclaim, *"I am no longer a descendant of Adam, I am a descendant of Christ. As far as I am concerned the Adamic-Lineage of sin is already dead, and I no longer identify with it. I no longer miss the mark, for the mark is in Christ Jesus."* The apostle Paul conformed, *"**I press toward the mark** for the prize of the high calling of God **in Christ Jesus**..."* (Phil 3:14). The practical implications of this confession is that I need not be focused on becoming righteous, because in Christ I am already righteous with God's perfect righteousness! All there remains for me to do, is to grow up in my already obtained righteousness, to become a mature Son of God.

> » *In 'Confessing Christ and Denying the Flesh,' we confess the characteristics of the Christ-Lineage as being true concerning ourselves, while denying and rejecting the characteristics of the Adamic-Lineage.*

In confessing my belief in the opinion of God, I am exercising Faith. Faith is having confidence in God's Character, Ability and Promises to bring to pass the Christ-Lineage from within. Faith is believing and receiving God's opinion of me, which is really based on His opinion of Jesus. Faith is allowing my identity to be informed and formed by God's opinion of me.

My Relationship to God – In Adam versus In Christ

My opinion of God changed when I believed in His true opinion of me. As a result, my relationship toward God experienced a complete transformation. As in any relationship, we tend to relate to someone on the basis of how we think they perceive us. If we think that a person hates us, we tend to avoid them. We would not trust such a person. However, if we think that a person loves us, we tend to trust that person and seek their company.

Once more I will list a few contrasting aspects of the relationship between God and a person *'in Adam'* versus a person *'in Christ.'* Keep in mind, God's opinion has never changed, the change in relationship comes when that person believes the truth about God's opinion.

Relationship to God in Adam	Relationship to God in Christ
Separated from God (Eph 2:12)	**One with God** (John 17:21; Matt 10:40; John 14:23)
Slaves (Gal 4:7)	**Sons of God** (John 1:12; Gal 4:7; 1John 3:2; Rom 8:16)
Enemies (Rom 5:10)	**Friends (Reconciled)** (Rom 5:10; John 15:15)

Governed by External Law / Under Laws written in Ink and Tables of Stone (Romans 7:1; 2 Cor 3:7; 1Tim 1:9)	Dead to the Law / Governed by the Spirit of the Living God written in the Tables of the Heart (Rom 7:4,6; 2 Cor 3:3; Ezek 36:27; Rom 13:9-10)
Bears Fruit Unto Death (Romans 7:5)	Brings Forth Fruit unto God (Romans 7:4)
Oldness of Letter which Kills *(Can't give Life)* (Romans 7:6)	Newness of Spirit which Gives Life (Romans 7:6)
Condemnation, Death (2 Cor 3:7, 9)	Justification, Life (2 Cor 3:6; John 17:3)
Cannot Inherit the Kingdom of God (1Cor 15:50)	Inherits the Kingdom of God (Jas 2:5; Matt 25:34)

This table, as well as the previous one, helps us to see the devastation caused by humanity's choice of the Tree of the Knowledge of Good and Evil. The fruit of that tree continues to poison the minds even of Christians who profess to know the truth. Many simply cannot believe that this is the truth. They may be willing to accept the thought of Jesus dying for our sins, for this is in line with the opinion of a God who wants us to perform lists of moral Do's and Don'ts to make us more like Him. So the idea of Christ dying to give us a temporary reprieve from our slips on our way up the ladder to heaven, doesn't require a change in our distorted opinion of God.

But for many, the idea that God actually views us as His Friends and wants to have an intimate, trusting relationship with us, cannot be received. God to many Christians remains a Master, not a Father. Thus many Christians, *even though they may call God 'Father,'* continue to relate to God as slaves, and not as sons. What is the difference you may ask? Here is a simple, yet applicable example.

A powerful king has a son and a servant. Let us tabulate their respective relationships with the king.

Servant (Slave)	Son
Is of a different lineage, related by employment	Is of the same lineage as the king, related by blood
Accepted by the king through employment, to perform a specific task	Accepted by the king because he is his son
Is on probation due to mistakes and failures	Is loved regardless of mistakes and failures
Remains employed as long as performance is maintained	Is always the king's son regardless of performance
Is only the steward of the king's possessions. Eventually might be employed by the son	Inherits all the king's possessions because he is the king's son

Notice that even though the servant may enjoy some benefits of being employed by a king, they are in no way comparable to the blessings of being the king's son. Notice the servant's acceptance is performance-based, while the son's acceptance is blood-based. The servant, no matter how excellent his service may be, will always be a servant. The son however, remains the king's son no matter how many failures and mistakes he commits. Whether we consider this to be fair or not, this is the way it is. Fallen humanity's default relationship to God is that of Slave-to-Master. Only when the true opinion of God is received, then humanity transitions to the relationship of Son-to-Father. The apostle Paul agrees with this principle, *"the spiritual **was not first**, but the natural; then the spiritual."* (1Cor 15:46). Paul was describing the transition of humanity's identity – from natural to spiritual. The natural comes first in sequence and the spiritual last. But in terms of God's way, *the preferred one is the last* – the spiritual. Likewise, fallen humanity must transition from the first state of Servant to the last of Son. The Left Column of the table illustrates the way a natural man (Servant) relates to God, while the Right Column reflects the way a spiritual man (Son) relates to God. According to how you view God – as Master or Father, your identity manifests accordingly.

Confessing the truth of God's opinion of you seems to be too good to be true, for God is indeed Too Good! He Himself de-clared, *"For as the heavens are higher than the earth, so are my ways higher than your ways, and my thoughts than your thoughts!"* (Isa 55:9)

I remember when I first began to confess my In-Christ relation-ship to God, tears gushed forth from my eyes, as a tremendous weight was lifted from my soul. Yes, it was true! In Christ, I am One with my Father, I am His Son and His Friend! No longer am I an enemy, a slave – separated from Him by the fruit of the Tree of the Knowledge of Good and Evil. In Christ and through Christ, I have been brought to the Tree of Life having received God's true opinion of me.

I sincerely encourage you to go through the two tables presented – that of the Lineage and of the Relationship, and confess your In-Christ identity, pondering each characteristic as made clear by the scripture references. I guarantee you, the experience is mind-blowing!

Daily we should capture every thought, which, like the serpent in the Garden, seek to convince us to receive our identity from the Tree of the Knowledge of Good and Evil. I have found that the depressing and discouraging thoughts always agree with the paradigm of the Tree of the Knowledge of Good and Evil. Uplifting, positive, encouraging and creative thoughts always originate from the Tree of Life. Make it a practice of analyzing our thoughts to ascertain their origin. If they are from the Tree of the Knowledge of Good and Evil, instantly deny them and counter them with the truth from the Tree of Life. The apostle counseled that *"we destroy arguments and every lofty opinion raised against the knowledge of God, and **take every thought captive to obey Christ**..."* (2Cor 10:5). Vigorously deny those satanic lies, and dispel them with the opinion of God concerning our identity in Christ!

'Confessing Christ and Denying the Flesh' should be a moment-by-moment daily practice, until it becomes automatic. We are to continuously keep our minds on the paradigm of the Tree of Life. The apostle Paul advised, *"whatever is true, whatever is honorable, whatever is fair, whatever is pure, whatever is acceptable, whatever is commendable, if there is anything of excellence and if there is anything praiseworthy—**keep thinking about these things**."* (Phil 4:8). Let us keep foremost in our thoughts our glorious identity in Christ. Let us see ourselves as God sees us, for truly in God's eyes we are true, honorable, fair, pure, acceptable, commendable, excellent and praiseworthy!

CHAPTER 14
Sabbathkeeping - How to Rest in Your Identity

God rested at the Creation

According to the narrative, God had created humanity in six days and rested on the seventh day. When I examined the account of the days of creation, I discovered that the end of each day was concluded with the demarcation, *"And the evening and the morning were the first day; ...second day; ...third day; ...fourth day; ...fifth day; ...sixth day."* (Gen 1:5, 8, 13, 19, 23, 31)

However, the account of the seventh day was not punctuated with this demarcation. In other words, the author of Genesis did not record: *"and the evening and the morning were the seventh day."* There must be a reason why the writer departed from his established pattern of demarcating the days. Instead, the author wrote, *"And on the seventh day God ended his work which he had made; and he rested on the seventh day from all his work which he had made."* (Gen 2:2)

As I pondered on why there was no demarcation of the seventh day as was done for the previous six, it occurred to me that on the seventh day God had *ended* His work. God did not intend to resume working the following week. As far as God was concerned, He had finished working, His creation was complete, and it required no further modification. So when God rested on the seventh day, He intended to rest forever. That seventh day in reality would have no end, because God had finished working, and had begun resting, not for a 24-hour period, but for all time. This is why I believe the author did not demarcate the seventh day as having ended. It was because God's rest was to be eternal – without end. Thus, when God *"blessed the seventh day, and sanctified it,"* (Gen 2:3) He was blessing not a 24-hour period, but His eternal, never-ending rest. This is what I call the Creation Sabbath.

» *As far as God was concerned, He had finished working, His creation was complete, and it required no further modification. So when God rested on the seventh day, He intended to rest forever*

Humanity at the creation also rested. They came forth from the hand of the creator toward the end of the sixth day. They opened their eyes in a world where everything that they could possibly need had already been put in place. Everything was already provided, and in super-abundance. They were crowned with honor and glory, a little lower than God, in His presence, filled with joy and pleasure. They did not have to work for any of this. They simply received all of it as evidence of God's love toward them. And they rested in all of it. Thus, humanity's rest in God's love and provision was also to have been for all time. They were to rest forever in their identity, and in God's opinion of them. That rest was not to be a 24-hour period of time, but an eternal moment-by-moment appreciation of the love of God towards them. Thus humanity entered into the Creation Sabbath rest by their Faith in God.

Fast-forward to the encounter at the Tree of the Knowledge of Good and Evil. When humanity ate the fruit of this tree, they ceased to rest in God. They no longer trusted God. They no longer believed that He loved them unconditionally and desired their good. They no longer believed that they were worthy of being Gods. From that point they no longer were experiencing the Creation Sabbath. In crippling fear they hid themselves from the presence of God. The terror they felt toward Him ensured that they could never experience rest.

God honored humanity's choice to be under the paradigm of the Tree of the Knowledge of Good and Evil. But He too had to cease resting and began working to rescue humanity from its horrific choice. Jesus confirmed this when he said, *"My Father is working until now, and I am working,"* (John 5:17). God's original creation had become marred. The True character of God was largely hidden from man, not because God wanted it to be so, but because of humanity's unbelief. The curse of the Tree of the Knowledge of Good and Evil was reigning. The scripture said, *"death reigned from Adam until Moses…"* (Rom 5:14). God had instituted a system of Knowledge of Good and Evil called Law, which was a ministry of the curse of death. The spirit showed that *"**the ministry of death**, having been **engraved in letters on stones**, was produced in glory…"* (2Cor 3:7). He put humanity under this system, according to Adam's choice. The apostle Paul wrote, *"before the faith came, **we were being kept-in-custody under the Law** — being confined until the faith destined to be revealed. So then the Law has been our tutor leading to Christ…"* (Gal 3:23-24). The Law had given humanity a taste of the results of the Tree of the Knowledge of Good and Evil. When Christ came, humanity should have gladly welcomed the opportunity to eat from the Tree of Life. Unfortunately, many seemed to prefer the old way. As Jesus observed, *"No one who has been drinking old wine would suddenly desire new wine, because he says, '**The old wine is good enough!**'"* (Luke 5:39)

God had ceased His rest and had been working to bring a redeemer into the world – the Promised Seed who would undo the damage done by Adam. He chose the Israelite people as the means through which this redeemer would come. The scripture revealed, *"the promises were spoken to Abraham and to **his**"*

seed. *It does not say 'and to seeds' as of many but 'and to your seed' as of One, who is Christ,"* (Gal 3:16). Christ, the redeemer, would be the seed from which would spring forth a new line of humanity. He would begin a new creation that was delivered from the curse of the Tree of the Knowledge of Good and Evil. The apostle Paul wrote, *"Christ redeemed us from the **curse of the Law**, having become a curse for us — for it has been written: '**Cursed is everyone hanging on a Tree...**'"* (Gal 3:13). In the meantime, humanity had been given 4,000 years – from Adam to Christ – to experience first-hand the results of choosing the Tree of the Knowledge of Good and Evil.

Within the system of Law, God placed ceremonies that were signs and symbols of what He intended to accomplish with His Redeemer, the New Adam. Among these signs was the 4th Commandment, which was a requirement for Israelites to abstain from work, or to rest for a 24-hour period, every seventh day. According to the bible narrative, God instructed Israel to *"consecrate my sabbaths; and **they were for a sign** between me and between you to know that I am Jehovah your God..."* (Ezek 20:20). This 24-hour period of rest was a *sign or a symbol* in memory of the original Creation Sabbath, in which God and humanity had rested. A sign by definition is not the real thing, but always *points* to the real thing. God had instructed the Israelites, *"the seventh day is the sabbath of the LORD your God: in it you shall not do any work, ...**for in six days the LORD made** heaven and earth, the sea, and all that in them is, **and rested the seventh day,"*** (Exod 20:10-11). This 24-hour period was only a commemoration of the real rest that God and humanity had originally enjoyed before Sin interrupted it. This enforced rest was the *shadow* of the eternal rest that God had been working to reinstate when the new creation would be finished. The scripture confirmed, *"the sabbath days... are **a shadow of things to come**; but the body is of Christ..."* (Col 2:16-17).

When the fullness of time came, God sent forth the Last Adam. The way of the Tree of the Knowledge of Good and Evil was about to be judged. 2,000 years ago Jesus had announced, *"Now is the judgment of this world..."* (John 12:31). The way of the Tree of the Knowledge of Good and Evil was condemned. It was shown to be the way of the Serpent, the one who had recommended it to humanity in the first place. That is why in that judgment the serpent was also judged, as Jesus had declared, *"the ruler of this world **has been judged**..."* (John 16:11).

Here is what that judgment revealed:

- A distorted belief of God's opinion leads one to fight against those who believed His True Opinion.

- Lists of moral Do's and Don'ts did not prevent humanity from distrusting God's Character, Ability and Promises.

- Lists of moral Do's and Don'ts did not prevent humanity from murdering its creator, redeemer and savior.

- What humanity needs are not lists of moral Do's and Don'ts, but a real living connection to God.

- What humanity needs is the revelation of God's true opinion of humanity, as demonstrated in the person of Jesus Christ.

The Tree of the Knowledge of Good and Evil was instrumental in the murder of the Last Adam. God, however, resurrected *"the Author of life..."* (Acts 3:15) as *"the Beginning of God's [new] creation..."* (Rev 3:14). Jesus is the fulfillment of the Tree of Life, and now invites humanity to *"come to **Me**, that you may have **Life!**"* (John 5:40). In the Revelation of Jesus, we see that anyone who was overcoming in Christ, God *"will give to him to eat of the Tree of Life..."* (Rev 2:7). It is essential to eat of that Tree of Life, as Christ said *"the one eating my flesh and drinking my blood has eternal life..."* (John 6:54) and *"the one eating My flesh and drinking My blood **abides in Me, and I in him**..."* (John 6:56). The flesh of Christ represented his humanity and his blood represented his life, or his spirit. What ever we consume becomes part of us, or one with us. Christ, as the Tree of Life, was inviting us to be one with him – he in us and we in him. We are to assume his freely given identity as ours, that his eternal Life should be integrated into us. This is what is needed to overcome the paradigm of the Tree of the Knowledge of Good and Evil. The apostle John reinforced the teaching of overcoming that dark paradigm, when he wrote, *"who is the one overcoming the world, except the one trusting that Jesus is the Son of God?"* (1John 5:5). It is crucial that we always remember that when we believe that Jesus was the Son of God, we are actually believing that *we are Sons of God*. This was why Jesus emphasised his identity as *'Son of Humanity.'* As the Son of Humanity, he was letting us know that he was one of us, and as Son of God, he has made Sons of Humanity into Sons of God.

God has rested once more, at His New Creation

Now that the New Adam has come, there has been a new creation. The scriptures affirm, *"Therefore if anyone is in Christ, **he is a new creation**..."* (2Cor 5:17). Since there is a new creation, we know that God is once more resting, not for a weekly 24-hour period, but for eternity. Thus, the rest which the weekly 24-hour observance was a shadow of, has now been here for the past 2,000 years. Jesus pleads, *"Come to Me, all the ones being weary and having been burdened, **and I will give you rest!"***

(Matt 11:28)

The rest that Jesus offers is not the weekly 24-hour sign, but what that old sign pointed to – the eternal New Creation Rest. The apostle said, *"for whoever has entered God's rest has also rested from his works as God did from His..."* (Heb 4:10). We are counseled to rest *like God did!* God is resting, not for a 24-hour period, but for eternity. The work that He has done through the Last Adam is perfect and needs neither modification nor improvement. He has provided all things abundantly in Christ. We are told, ***"His divine power has granted to us all things that pertain to life and godliness... He has granted to us his precious and very great promises***, *so that through them* ***you may become partakers of the divine nature..."*** (2Pet 1:3-4). Here God has given to humanity Exceeding Great and Precious promises that are concerning the *Divine Nature* – our True Identity as Gods. I am sure that these promises seem too good to be true, because indeed, God is too good, yet He is true. But, what will be our response? Would it be one of Faith or one of Unbelief?

If our response to these Wonderfully Impossible promises is a response of Faith, then we rest in our confidence in God's Character and Ability to bring those Exceeding Great and Precious promises into our reality. We then enter into the Creation Sabbath rest like Adam and Eve did before their fall. But if our response is one of Unbelief, then we remain in the identity of Adam and Eve *after the Fall*, under the curse of the Tree of the Knowledge of Good and Evil. We would wander in the wilderness of this existence, until we perish.

I have chosen to rest in God's New Creation. My rest is not the weekly 24-hour sign, but the moment-by-moment reality. I have chosen to accept His opinion of me. I have found my identity, and it is too good, yet True!

CHAPTER 15
How to Defeat the Spirit of Doubt

Like humanity in the beginning, we can expect to be tested by the enemy concerning our identity. This is why God had Jesus go through a 'do-over' of the testing of the First Adam. According to the narrative, *"then Jesus was led up into the wilderness by the spirit **to be tested by the Adversary**..."* (Matt 4:1) What was this test all about? We remember the testing of humanity at the beginning. They were tested concerning God's opinion of them. Since Jesus was the Last Adam, he too must be tested concerning God's opinion of him. What was God's opinion of Jesus? Just one verse before, the narrative recorded God's opinion of Jesus, *"This is my Son, **the Beloved, in whom I delight!**"* (Matt 3:17)

As soon as Jesus was given this heavenly affirmation of his identity, along with God's positive opinion of him, *"straightway the spirit drives him into the wilderness. And He was in the wilderness forty days, **undergoing trial by the Adversary**..."* (Mark 1:12-13). Here we see that the New Adam was being tested, and we suspect that this test was along the same line as the First Adam, concerning God's opinion of him. Let us examine the course of attack the enemy chose against Jesus.

Jesus' Battle with Doubt

*"And the tester comes to him, and says, '**If you are the Son of God**, command that these stones become bread!'"* (Matt 4:3). Don't miss the test. Forty days ago, Jesus had heard God's opinion of him: *"This is my Son, the Beloved, in whom I delight!"* Now, hungry and malnourished from forty days without food, did he still believe that?

The enemy's attack was calculated to cause Jesus to doubt that he was indeed the Son of God. *"If you were really the Son of God, you wouldn't be starving in this wilderness. Come on, turn these stones to bread if you are really the Son of God!"* We can see that as soon as Jesus was given God's opinion concerning his identity, he was immediately tested on his faith in that opinion. If Jesus had heeded the adversary's provocation, he would have fallen victim of the Tree of the Knowledge of Good and Evil. We recall that humanity in the Garden partook of the forbidden tree, after they had succumbed to the lie that they would *"be like Gods..."* Humanity had already been made in the likeness of God. There was nothing that they needed to do concerning that likeness. However, the serpent had succeeded in corrupting their self-awareness and self-perception, causing them to desire to eat of the forbidden tree *to be like God*. They had therefore come to perceive themselves as being not like God. *Thus their perception became their reality.* They had allowed another opinion other than God's opinion, to inform and form their self-awareness and self-perception. They then believed that they needed to do something *to make themselves be like God!*

Likewise, the adversary's attack on the identity of Jesus carried the same poison: *"you need to turn stones to bread if you are really the Son of God!"* If Jesus had attempted to do a miracle to prove that he was the Son of God, it would have been an act of Unbelief. Such an action would have shown that he had no trust in his Father's Character, Ability and Promises. It was the Father who had identified him as His Son. Put another way, he was the Son of God, *because the Father said so!* It was the Father who had affirmed His delight in him. There was absolutely no need to do anything to 'prove' this anyone, not even himself. God's opinion is to be received by Faith.

As weak as he was from the lack of food, he was having none of the enemy's suggestions of doubt. Jesus responded to the spirit of doubt, *"Not on bread alone shall man be living, but on **every declaration going out from the mouth of God!**"* (Matt 4:4) The declaration that had proceeded out of his Father's mouth just 40 days ago was: *"This is my Son, the Beloved, in whom I delight!"* Jesus chose to exercise Faith in his Father's declaration. It was his Faith in his Father's opinion of him that sustained Jesus throughout his suffering in the wilderness. It was Faith in those words that succeeded in banishing the spirit of doubt from his presence. According to the narrative, ***"Then the adversary leaves him,*** *and behold, angels came and were ministering to him."* (Matt 4:11)

We must overcome the spirit of Doubt

The spirit of Doubt will likewise come to snatch away our true identity from us. In fact, like Jesus, we must be tested on whether or not we truly believe God's wonderful opinion about us. In Christ, we too are God's Beloved Sons in whom He delights. In Christ, we are the new creation, of which God has declared we are very Good. In Christ, we are friends of God, one with God and blameless.

The adversary's attack will seek to fix our focus on any unpleasant circumstance we may be experiencing. He seeks to get our attention unto our difficulties and not on God's affirmation. He seeks to get us to doubt our true identity because of whatever uncomfortable situation we may be in. *"If you were really God's Son, you would not be in such a predicament. Do something to prove that you are really God's Son!"*

The attacks of the enemy are relentless, and as varied as the sand of the sea, but are unanimous in their objective – to make you doubt the Word of God concerning your identity. *"You cannot be God's Begotten Child, partaking of the divine nature, because that would be presumptuous, because you are a sinner, because...because...because..."* You can fill in blanks with whatever doubts the tempter is speaking to you. But like Abraham and Jesus, we must not look at the unpleasantness nor impossibility of our circumstance. Instead, we are to look at God's wonderful opinion, we are to believe His glorious affirmation – *"You are my Beloved Sons in whom I delight!"*

We did not obtain our true identity by theft, but at the authority given to us by God. We can only but believe this exceeding great and precious declaration. We cannot make ourselves God's beloved offspring. But God declared that He has begotten us by His Spirit. We should be able to say to the spirit of Doubt: *"I am God's Beloved Child, because He says I am! Get thee behind me, Satan!"*

The spirit of Doubt would seek to point out to you that if you were really God's Begotten Child you would be able to work great miracles. This is true in a sense, because Jesus did say: *"Verily, verily, I say unto you, He that believes on me, the works that I do shall he do also; and greater works than these shall he do; because I go unto my Father..."* (John 14:12). Jesus declared that *"the Father, remaining in Me, He is doing His works..."* (John 14:10). Therefore, all that are in Christ have the power of the Father within. However, learning to access that power through works of faith is something that comes with time. Understand, even if you have never done one thing that would seem miraculous, *it does not change, nor define, whom God says you are!* Our identity is not based on what we do, but on whom God says we are! Nonetheless, there is one great work that we can do, which Jesus revealed in his conversation with the super-righteous Pharisees of his time.

> » *All that are in Christ have the power of the Father within.*
> *However, learning to access that power through works of*
> *faith is something that comes with time.*

The Pharisees had asked him, *"What must we do, that we may be doing the works of God?"* Jesus answered them, ***"This is the work of God, that you should believe in him whom He has sent!"*** (John 6:28-29). Notice what is the work of God that we are to do – to Believe in Jesus! The Pharisees were under the paradigm of the Tree of the Knowledge of Good and Evil, so they believed that they could do things to become like God. They saw Jesus' effortless Godlikeness, and wondered what more laws did they need to perform to achieve such an exalted way of life. However, Jesus let them know there is no law given to make us like God, only God can make humanity in His Likeness! Therefore the only way to work the works of God, is to believe and receive what He has provided. The paradigm of the Tree of the Knowledge of Good and Evil is *'doing;'* the paradigm of the Tree of Life is *'believing and receiving.'* Our work is to believe in the New Adam – Jesus, in whose lineage we inherit all of his spiritual genetics. Our work is to have faith in the Father's opinion of Jesus, which is His opinion of us! Our work is to believe that Jesus' Father is our Father. In Christ, we are of the same spiritual DNA as him! Jesus made this stunning declaration to his disciples after his resurrection, *"I am ascending to **My Father and your Father!**"* (John 20:17). Yes, in Christ, God is the Father of us and Jesus! We inherit all His divine attributes and we are His offspring in whom He delights!

So we should be able to say to the spirit of Doubt, *"I believe that I am God's beloved offspring because I am working the Works of God. I believe in Jesus whom my Father has sent. And I believe the promise that he has made that I have authority from God to be His beloved Son! Get thee behind me, Satan!"*

Be bold in your identity, for you are not trusting in your own opinion, but in God's opinion of you. This faith is like that of Abraham and Sarah when they conceived Isaac, the kind that is rewarding.

CHAPTER 16
The First Commandment

The Commandments of the Kingdom of Heaven were given for those who have received God's true opinion. Once that opinion was received, no longer would they perceive themselves as slaves, servants and employees of God, but as Sons, Children and Offspring of God. With this new birth, they are ready to walk in the Commandments of the Kingdom of Heaven, *"and **this is His commandment**, that we should **have faith in the name of His Son Jesus Christ, and love one another**, as he gave us Commandment."* (1John 3:23). Here are given the two Great Commandments of the Kingdom of Heaven. They are:

1. Have faith in the name of God's Son Jesus Christ.

2. Love one another.

These two Commandments as we shall see, are all that Sons of God need to guide them in living their true identity. Let's look at the First Commandment in this chapter, and the Second in the next.

Have faith in the name of God's Son – Jesus Christ

By now you may have noticed, the majority of this book is in harmony with the First Commandment, the goal of having faith in the name of God's Son – Jesus Christ. What is the importance of having faith in the *name*? Anyone familiar with the scriptures should come to the realization that names are important and significant. In terms of humanity, there were several great names in the scriptures. We can easily think of names like Adam, Noah, Abraham, Isaac, Jacob/Israel, Judah, Moses, David, Solomon and of course Jesus. What we may notice is that these great men's names carried such prestige, that their generations were surnamed after them. We can think of the biblical families: *'Sons of Adam,' 'Children of Israel,' 'House of Israel,'* and *'Judeans'* (Jews, the sons of Judah). These men's names lived on through their descendants. Those descendants were often afforded favor because of the ancestor's name. For example, God frequently acted on the behalf of Abraham's descendants because of the relationship that He and Abraham had possessed. It was because of Abraham's name that his descendants were favored.

In other instances, a name afforded authority and prestige. The prophets of God were all sent *'in the name of the Lord.'* God said concerning the ministry of a prophet, *"he shall speak unto them all that I shall command him. And it shall come to pass, that whosoever will not hearken unto my words which the prophet shall speak **in my name**, I will require it of that man."* (Deut 18:18-19). Thus God's prophets were empowered to act and speak *in his name*, on his behalf. Thus, they were to be afforded the same respect as God, and feared with the same fear.

It is these two aspects of the name of Jesus Christ that we are called to have faith in – the inherited favor, and the authority and prestige. Jesus Christ is God's favored and beloved Son, in whom He delights. The apostle John said of Jesus, he was *"an only begotten from the Father, **full of favor** and truth..."* (John 1:14). God has put Christ *"at His right hand in the heavenly realms, above every principality and authority and power and dominion, and every name being named... And He put all things under his feet..."* (Eph 1:20-22).

In my true identity as Son of God, I am placed in the name of

Jesus Christ – the new Adam. Even more precisely I am placed *in Christ*. Thus I am placed in the same beloved-ness, favor and prestige as Jesus, as long as I believe it! In fact, God commands me to believe it is so! If I fail to believe God's opinion concerning me, I am in disobedience to Him, and would have thwarted His divine will for me.

» *In my true identity as Son of God, I am placed in the name of Jesus Christ – the new Adam. Even more precisely I am placed in Christ. Thus I am placed in the same beloved-ness, favor and prestige as Jesus, as long as I believe it! In fact, God commands me to believe it is so!*

In the name of Jesus Christ I have favor, and I have authority and prestige. In the name of Jesus, I have favor with God and men. In this name God acts on our behalf, and even causes the negative and evil circumstances to turn out in our favor. In Jesus' name we have authority over sicknesses, destructive habits and behaviors. In his name we can effect positive change in negative environments. In his name we are freed from superstitious fear, religious traditions and ceremonies.

The name of Jesus Christ is our covenantal birth name, for we are born into Christ, thus we bear his name as his own family. As members of his family, we have the access that he has, the favor that he has, the authority that he has and the prestige that he has. Everything we do and purpose to do, must be done with our identity in Christ as its foundation. Every situation and circumstance that presents itself to us, must be viewed through this lens. As God's offspring, we have been given His true opinion of us, and should never allow trying circumstances to sway our belief in that opinion. Even when faced with peril, we must always remember, that God loves us with all of His being and never changes His opinion. The apostle Paul wrote, *"For I am sure* *that neither death nor life, nor angels nor rulers, nor things present nor things to come, nor powers, nor height nor depth, nor anything else in all creation, will be able to separate us **from the love of God in Christ Jesus our Lord**."* (Rom 8:38-39)

This is why we need to fortify our minds with the Confessions listed in the chapter *'Confessing Christ and Denying the Flesh.'* Our minds must be immersed with the understanding, *"I am in Christ, I am favored like Christ, I am empowered with his power."* The apostle counsels us that *"...anything that is not of faith is sin."* (Rom 14:23). In the Kingdom of Heaven our mark is Jesus. So when we fail to have faith in his name and all the benefits afforded us by that name, we are missing the mark – or are sinning. We must never allow the spirit of doubt or fear to even suggest that the finished work that God accomplished in Christ is not enough for us; that there is something that we need to add to that work to perfect it. We must not allow the adversary to cause us to think that God has let go of us, or that we may have gone beyond his reach. We must face every obstacle, with the firm trust that *'in Christ'* every mountain is either removed or made low. This is the Commandment that God has given to His Sons. Do not stop trusting in the name given to you, the name of Jesus Christ into which you were placed in the Christ-lineage. Apart from that name, you would still be in the name of Adam – condemned, and destined for the dirt.

CHAPTER 17
The Second Commandment

God has rescued me from my misinformed belief of His opinion of me. I have received His true opinion of me. That opinion now informs and forms my self-awareness and self-perception. He has restored me to the Tree of Life. It now remains for me to live out that opinion in everyday life. How should my new identity influence my interactions with others? Jesus, the one who had perfect confidence in his God-given identity, lived by one great principle – that of Love. He is remembered as saying to his disciples, *"a new commandment I give to you, that you should love one another. As I have loved you, so you also should love one another."* (John 13:34)

In the past, I supposed that Jesus had been quoting a long-forgotten commandment from the Law. After all, in the Law, it was written, *"You shall not avenge, nor bear any grudge against the children of your people, but **you shall love your neighbor as yourself**..."* (Lev 19:18). Again, Jesus, speaking to the Jews, told them: *"You shall love your neighbor as yourself."* (Matt 22:39)

Therefore, I assumed that he was simply restating that old commandment from the Law. But if that was the case, why then did he specifically say that it was *'a new commandment'*? On closer inspection of what Jesus said, I began to see that indeed he was speaking of a really NEW commandment. Let's look at it again. *"a **new commandment** I give to you, that you should love one another. **As I have loved you**, so you also should love one another."*

Did you notice the newness? The newness is in the *kind* of love that this commandment prescribes, it speaks of the *way* Jesus loved. Let us compare the old commandment with the new.

- OLD: *"you shall love your neighbor __as yourself__..."*

- NEW: *"__As I have loved you__, so you also should love one another."*

Notice the standard for the old commandment is 'Yourself.' However, the new standard was the divine Love. Before the advent of Christ, fallen humanity had no perfect guide of the love of God. Humanity therefore could not demonstrate the divine Love; they did not bear the likeness of the divine, because they believed they were not like God. They thought that God no longer loved them, and perceived themselves as not worthy of His love. As a result of this corrupted self-perception they could not love God nor each other. Lists of moral Do's and Don'ts had to be enforced upon them to govern their actions (works) toward God and each other. All of this was as a result of humanity's choice of the Tree of the Knowledge of Good and Evil.

Fallen humanity had become selfish. This is the opposite of God's nature, but because they perceived God as selfish, and they thought He was selfish toward them, they too became selfish toward each other. Thus the nature of fallen humanity is to love itself above all others. The Old Commandment used fallen humanity's best-known love – *Self Love* – as the standard of how humanity was commanded to love, *"you shall love your neighbor __as yourself__..."* The New Commandment, however, has a higher revelation of love – the divine Love of the Father revealed in the death of His Son on our behalf – *"**Greater love** has no one than this, that one should lay down his life for his friends..."* (John 15:13). In the life and death of Jesus, God's true opinion of mankind, as well as His character, power and promises were revealed as manifesting His love toward humanity.

> » *The Old Commandment used fallen humanity's best-known love – Self Love – as the standard of how humanity was commanded to love, "you shall love your neighbor as your-self..." The New Commandment, however, has a higher revelation of love – the divine Love of the Father revealed in the death of His Son on our behalf...*

For 4,000 years, fallen humanity under the paradigm of the Tree of the Knowledge of Good and Evil, did not have a revelation of the divine love of the Father! They had labored under the misconception of God's opinion of them. God for those millennia had sadly respected humanity's choice, and allowed Himself to be perceived in this evil way. However, there would come a time in which humanity would be ripe to receive the fullest manifestation of His divine love for them. When that time came, He sent His Son to live among humanity to reveal the truth about Himself.

Until that time, humanity could not be required to love each other *'as Jesus loved!'* The New Commandment could not be kept until after Jesus had come to demonstrate the Father's love for humanity. Jesus, as the Son of Humanity, manifested the divine love. This was because he was the only one to have seen (perceived, understood) the Father. He was the only one to have come from the Father, having been in His presence where there is fullness of joy and eternal pleasures at His right hand. He had the true opinion of God and he knew God's true opinion of humanity. Thus, a body was prepared for the Son of God, that he might bear this great revelation as the Son of Humanity.

Jesus was able to truly love all, because he knew that God loved all. Thus he counseled, *"love your enemies and pray for those persecuting you, so that you may be sons of your Father in the heavens. For He makes His sun rise on evil and good, and He sends rain on the righteous and unrighteous..."* (Matt 5:44-45). Jesus understood that Sons of God are like God. Only those who have received God's opinion of humanity can really love humanity. To really love, one has to see humanity through God's eyes. God views humanity as created worthy of His honor and glory. But through the evil spell of the fruit of the Tree of the Knowledge of Good and Evil, they are ignorant of their true dignity, clueless of their eternal worth, deceived concerning God's opinion of them and uninformed of the divine power that is available for them.

Humanity under the paradigm of the Tree of the Knowledge of Good and Evil had a distorted view of God's opinion of humanity. This distorted view, Jesus had to regularly correct among the Jews. There was the incident when a Samaritan village had not welcomed Jesus and his disciples. The disciples were indignant, and wanted fire from heaven to rain down on the villagers. Jesus rebuked them saying, *"You don't know of **what kind of spirit you are**. For the Son of Man didn't come to destroy men's lives, but to save them."* (Luke 9:55-56). Jesus understood that God was not a destroyer of humanity, but a loving healer and life-giver.

The apostle Paul's dissertation on the qualities of Love portrayed how God relates to humanity. He wrote, *"Love is patient, is kind. Love is not jealous. Love is not bragging, is not puffed up; it is not arrogant or rude. It does not insist on its own way; it is not irritable or resentful; it does not rejoice at injustice, but rejoices with the truth. Love is all-sustaining, all-believing, all-hoping, all-enduring."* (1Cor 13:4-7). Love, according to Paul, was *"a more excellent way..."* 1Cor 12:31. Under the inspiration of God's Spirit, Paul was able to see God's humble and tender heart for humanity, which in turn influenced Paul's earnestness in preaching the gospel of the kingdom to all Israel. God has been revealed as loving and kind, humble, gentle, ever-patient and encouraging. These are not the traditional ways of seeing God. Many Christians still speak of God as He was portrayed in the paradigm of the Tree of the Knowledge of Good and Evil. They praise Him as being a *"man of war..."* (Exod 15:3)

On the other hand, Jesus clearly identified the adversary as the destroyer, the same one who from the beginning had recommended the way of the Tree of the Knowledge of Good and Evil. On the contrary, Christ's mission was in harmony with the Tree of Life. He said, ***"the Thief*** *is not coming except that* ***he should be stealing*** *and* ***sacrificing*** *and* ***destroying.*** ***I came that they may have life eternal****, and have it superabundantly..."* (John 10:10). From this we see that the ultimate expression of God's love toward us is the enhancement of humanity's quality of life, through the knowledge of the truth of His opinion.

As Sons of God, we are the channels of God's wonderful love for humanity. Our Father's nature is to freely give. The Apostle James wrote, *"Every good act of giving and every perfect gift is from above, coming down from the Father of lights..."* (Jas 1:17). There is something about the giving of a gift to someone. Their spirit is filled with joy, which in turn fills us with joy. In this we know that we are fulfilling our true identity, being like our Father.

It should be our highest goal to patiently and kindly, by our prayers, deeds and words, lead everyone in our sphere of influence to this great knowledge of God's true opinion of humanity. This, in my opinion, is the greatest act of love that we can perform for anyone.

CHAPTER 18
I and My Father are One

*"I do not ask for these [Disciples] only, but **also for those believing in Me through their word**, that all may be one, as **you, Father, are in me, and I in you**, that they also may be in us, that the world may believe that you sent me. And I have given them the glory which you have given me, so **that they may be one, as we are one** — **I in them, and you in me** — that they may be completed in one..."* (John 17:20-23)

Jesus expressed his desire that those who believed in him would be brought into the same oneness that he had with his Father, the Only True God. This desire was not a whimsical dream nor a flight of fancy that Jesus wished could happen. On the contrary, he was fully confident in his Father's ability to do exactly what he had asked. Jesus knew that his Father was capable of uniting humanity's fallen spirit with His divine Spirit; that is why he asked his Father to accomplish his request. I believe that Jesus asked this incredible favor, based on two factors. The first was his faith in the Father's opinion of him: *"This is my Son, **the Beloved, in whom I delight!"*** (Matt 3:17). There was no way that the Father would deny this request made by his beloved Son. The second factor was, according to the promise that *"...**whatsoever we may be requesting, we are obtaining from Him**, for we are keeping His precepts and are doing what is pleasing in His sight..."* (1John 3:22). Jesus had kept his Father's precepts and had been doing what pleased his Father. He confessed, *"I have kept the precepts of My Father and am remaining in His love..."* (John 15:10). These factors combine to assure me that Jesus met all the qualifications for answered prayer. Therefore I believe without a shadow of doubt that Jesus' request for divine oneness with me, has absolutely been answered by His Father. All who believe in Jesus' true identity and message would be brought into this marvelous reality of being at one with God and His Son.

When I considered what Jesus said, I pondered the awesomeness of his request. Let us look at the elements of this oneness. According to Jesus' prayer request, these are the specifics of the Oneness that he mentioned.

- The Father is in Jesus

- Jesus is in the Father

- They [Sons of God] are in the Father and Jesus

- Jesus had been given the Glory of the Father

- Jesus had given the Glory of the Father to them [the Sons of God]

- Jesus is in them [the Sons of God]

This seems at first to be a mind-bending puzzle. How could the Father be in Jesus, yet at the same time Jesus be in the Father? How could Jesus be in all those who are Sons of God while they at the same time be in the Father *and* Jesus? How can *three* persons – the Father, the Son and You – be *one*? Such difficulties arise when we fail to realize that Jesus is speaking not of a unity of objects, but a unity of spirits. Three objects united are still three objects. In the natural realm unity cannot be gained by addition; one plus one plus one equals three ($1+1+1=3$). However, in the spirit realm, a unity of three spirits yields one spirit. Unity in the realm of the spirit is gained by multiplication; one times one times one equals one ($1 \times 1 \times 1=1$).

I have found that a good way of understanding this is to think of

God as a vast ocean. This shouldn't be such a stretch, since the scriptures already use liquid symbolism to describe God. For example, Solomon says of God, *"...behold, heaven and the heaven of heavens **cannot contain you**; how much less this house which I have built!"* (2Chr 6:18). Jesus revealed that the Father is Spirit, which lets us know that He, like the ocean, is vast and shapeless. We also know that on the Day of Pentecost, the disciples were *filled* with God's Spirit, another property of liquid.

The metaphor of the Ocean

If we therefore use the metaphor of the ocean, we can assume that humanity is like the spray from the waves that crash against the shore. That spray consists of millions of tiny individual droplets, each varying slightly in size and shape. They were separated from the ocean by the violence of the wave action. They are suspended in the air for a brief period, such as the brief interval that humanity appears on the scene of earth. The apostle James wrote, *"What is your life? For **you are a mist that appears for a little time and then vanishes**."* (Jas 4:14)

Let us consider that Jesus was one such droplet that appeared on the scene. He, for the brief period of his *'Son of Humanity'* identity, or we may say, his droplet-existence, revealed to the other droplets that he was just like them, yet also he was just like the ocean. Until that time, the other droplets had assumed that they were quite unlike the ocean. As far as they could see, the ocean was vast and deep, blue and flat. There was sea-life in the ocean. Huge vessels sailed on its surface. At times the surface was troubled with tremendous swells. The droplets, on the other hand, saw themselves as individuals – self-contained, tiny, colorless, round, powerless, insignificant and separate from the ocean. They found it hard to believe that they were just like the ocean. They laughed at Jesus, and some said he blasphemed for thinking that he and the ocean were one. But Jesus insisted, *"the ocean is in me and I am in the ocean! If you believe that I and the ocean are one, you would discover that you too can be one with the ocean!"* After giving his message, Jesus was received back into the ocean from which he had come. As he had said, *"I came out from the Father and have come into the world. Again, I am leaving the world and am going to the Father."* (John 16:28)

Many of the droplets did not believe him, but a few did. The ones that didn't believe, evaporated in the heat of the sun. However, those that did believe, fell gently into the ocean, and became one with the ocean. They discovered that everything the ocean was, they were!

This is the way that I have come to see the oneness of God and His Sons. This is how the Father can be in Jesus and at the same time Jesus can be in the Father. As the droplet and the ocean are both water, likewise Jesus and his Father are both of the same substance, one divine Spirit. When we receive the good news of God's opinion, that we too are Spirit like him, we are able to fall gently into him and be swallowed up into his vast and deep love and power. We are in him and he is in us. The apostle wrote, *"he that is joined unto the Lord **is one spirit**..."* (1Cor 6:17). This one spirit is the oneness of God and our spirit in Christ Jesus. I believe this is not just an agreement of mind, such as the unity of opinions. I also believe this is a oneness accomplished by God sharing his divinity with me. It is *'I'* being brought into His divine nature. This is what the apostle Paul was talking about when he said, *"For in Him we live and in Him we move and in Him we are."* (Acts 17:28)

> » *When we receive the good news of God's opinion, that we too are Spirit like him, we are able to fall gently into him and be swallowed up into his vast and deep love and power. We are in him and he is in us. The apostle wrote, "he that is joined unto the Lord is one spirit..." (1Cor 6:17).*

Many Christians believe that this oneness is an unfulfilled promise still out of the reach of humanity. However Jesus was clear that the oneness that he had prayed for, would be a present living reality for any individual who was trusting in his word. *"If **anyone** should be loving me, he will be keeping my word, and my Father will be loving him, and **we shall be coming to him** and **making an abode with him...**"* (John 14:23). Jesus revealed that the dwelling place that he would go to prepare, was that oneness of himself, the Father and the believer in the spirit realm within. Anyone who desired that oneness, would be keeping Jesus' word – trusting in him as God's demonstration of our true identity. That trust would result in the Father (divinity) and the Son (identity) coming into the believer. *"Whoever shall confess that Jesus is the Son of God, **God abides in him, and he in God.**"* (1John 4:15)

The Sons manifest the personality of the Father

As a result of this oneness, the personality of my Father is manifested through me, His Son. Everything that the Son is, I am. Everything that my Father has, I have access to. Everything the Son has, I have been given. To the religious, this sounds offensive. Jesus often offended the super-religious of his day by speaking forth the Father's opinion of himself. When Jesus confessed his oneness with the Father, they were ready to kill him. According to the narrative, Jesus had said, *"'I and the Father are one.'* There-

fore the Jews took up stones again, that they might stone him. They answered him, 'You, being a man, make yourself God!'" (John 10:30-31,33). The Jews fully understood the implications of Jesus' statement. What they didn't grasp however was that Jesus did not make himself God, it was the Father who had made him God! Anyone born of God, must also be God, of the same family and spiritual DNA, so to speak. Paul used similar logic in reasoning with the men at Mar's Hill in Athens. He had argued, *"Therefore, being offspring of God, we ought not to consider Divinity to be like to gold or to silver or to stone, a graven thing of man's craft and imagination..."* (Acts 17:29). Paul's point was that if intelligent, sentient beings are God's offspring, then God's nature could not be of gold, silver and stone. These materials are lifeless and soulless, quite unlike God. God's children should bear His personality. Thus the reverse is also true. Since the Father is God – divine spirit, then His Sons would also be as He is – divine spirit. The apostle John proclaimed this good news in his epistle. He wrote, *"...just as He is, also are we in this world..."* (1John 4:17). The identity that God gives, inseparably links us to Him in all things. Jesus affirmed, *"The one receiving [the Sons of God] receives [the Son of God], and the one receiving me receives [the Father] who sent me!"* (Matt 10:40). This is the inherited prestige of being Sons of God. I bear His name wherever I go.

The seven 'I Am' affirmations of the Son of God

When we have received our true identity, we can begin to confess the qualities of that identity. Remember, every aspect has already been integrated into our new identity. All we need to do is put it on. In other words, we are not doing to become, but believing that we already are. Confession is the act of informing our inner Person and forming our Personality. Subsequently, from the inward invisible spirit, the visible 'works' would naturally manifest. Remember, when the Pharisees enquired, *"What must we do, that we may be doing the works of God?"* Jesus answered them, ***"This is the work of God, that you should believe in him whom He has sent!"*** (John 6:28-29). The work of God is to believe in the Christ identity that the Father has given you. This is the fundamental difference between religion and identity. Religion seeks to modify the outward. Identity forms from the inward. Once the inward is informed and formed, then the outward naturally manifests what is inward.

Jesus confessed seven aspects of his true identity. Do you realize that as Sons of God, we too should have the same confession as Christ? In fact, Jesus said, *"everyone who will confess in me before humanity, I also will confess in him before my Father in the heavens. And whoever shall deny me before humanity, I also will deny him before my Father in the heavens."* (Matt 10:32-33). If we examine this statement of Jesus, we can see that he was applying the principle of the invisible manifesting through the visible. Christ was instructing us to confess in our Christ Identity *'before humanity'*, i.e. in the presence of *our old identity*. Our inner Person needs to be informed that it is no longer *a son of fallen humanity*. We are letting ourselves know what is our true identity according to the opinion of God. We need to speak to ourselves the opinion of God. When we do this, Jesus (our true identity) confesses us in the presence of the Father in the heavens, the invisible realm, who makes our confession into fact. We see here a cooperation between God and us in the establishing of our true identity within the spirit realm. Once our identity is conceived in the inner invisible spirit realm, it will be brought forth in the visible natural realm. However, the converse is equally true. If we deny our Christ-identity, then such an identity cannot be conceived in the spirit, nor manifested in the natural.

113

With that said, let us see the seven *'I Am'* affirmations we are to confess as Sons of God.

1. *"I am the bread of life..."* (John 6:35). Jesus said, *"The one eating My flesh and drinking My blood **abides in Me, and I in him**..."* (John 6:56). In Christ, Sons of God are one with the Bread of Life, have become bread to those who are hungry for the true opinion of God concerning them. Many are captive in the fear-based ministry of death from the Tree of the Knowledge of Good and Evil. The bread of life is the living demonstration of the true opinion of God. It is the living witness of the freedom that Sons enjoy in Christ. In this affirmation, Sons thank the Father for making them to be the Living Bread that they may bring the life of God to humanity.

2. *"I am the light of the world..."* (John 8:12). Humanity is in a tragic darkness concerning the opinion of God. Sons of God are the light of the world. We are the visible manifestation of God's Truth and His Love. Jesus himself affirmed, *"You are the light of the world."* (Matt 5:14). In harmony with our Father's character of love, we bring forth from within us the light of God to every dark and dead soul we come in contact with. There is just *'something about us'* that turns every gloomy situation into one of hope. We are always positive and confident, trusting in the ability of our Father to work *'all things together for good.'* In this affirmation, Sons thank the Father for making them the Light for those who are in darkness, that they may help them to see the Light of Truth concerning God.

3. *"I am the door..."* (John 10:7,9). As Sons of God, we

have entered through Christ – the Door. We have become what we have entered through, we are made to be open doors, showing clearly the way to the Father to all who are seeking Him. We do not shut up the way to the Father, as religion does. Jesus rebuked the Pharisees because they *"shut up the kingdom of the heavens before men. For you neither enter, nor even do you allow those who are entering to go in..."* (Matt 23:13). As open doors to the Father, we remove the clutter of tradition, ceremony, fear and unbelief from the way, so the seeker has a clear entrance to the Father. We restore the *'key of knowledge'* to humanity. Jesus upbraided the teachers of Law of his day, *"you take away the key of knowledge;* **you yourselves do not enter, and those who are entering you prevent.**" (Luke 11:52) In this affirmation, Sons thank the Father for making them doors to Him, that they may show the way to the Father through their Christ identity.

4. *"I am the resurrection and the life..."* (John 11:25). In our Adamic identity, we had been *'dead in trespasses and missing the mark.'* The mark that was missed was the Christ identity. When we received the truth of God's opinion, we resurrected out from the paradigm of the Tree of the Knowledge of Good and Evil, unto God's Tree of Life; raised out from the kingdom of death, to the kingdom of Life. Thus Sons are the living embodiment of resurrection to eternal life. In this affirmation, Sons thank the Father for making them the resurrection and life, that they may give to others the Words of Life which in turn would raise them to eternal life.

5. *"I am the good shepherd..."* (John 10:11, 14). Sons of

God are good shepherds. This is a life of ministry to other Sons of God. A shepherd's role involves feeding the lambs and the sheep. This is the teaching ministry where we share among each other what we have learned from our Father. We are to go after the wandering ones. Many Sons need to socialize with and be edified by other Sons. A good shepherd is there for the sheep to provide meaningful fellowship and to protect each other from the deceptions of the adversary. Jesus told Peter, *"shepherd my sheep..."* (John 21:16) and *"strengthen your brothers..."* (Luke 22:32). In this affirmation, Sons thank the Father for making them good shepherds, that all Sons can be edified and supported by our ministry.

6. *"I am the way, the truth, and the life."* (John 14:6). Our Christ identity is the visible manifestation of all truth and knowledge about God's Opinion. In our identity resides the way to God, the Truth about God and the Eternal Abundant Life of God. Christ is the Way, and anyone in him becomes the Way as well. In the book of Acts, the believers in Christ were called *'The Way.'* It was recorded that Saul of Tarsus *"persecuted **This Way** as far as death, binding and betraying to prisons both men and women..."* (Acts 22:4). The Way is not to humanity's religious liturgy and ceremonies, but to the Father. That way is by being born from above as God's Sons. Therefore all Sons are His Way.

His Sons are born as a result of receiving the Spirit of Truth, making them the Sons of Truth – the Truth in living bodies. They have rejected the lies from the old paradigm and received the Truth of God's Opinion.

His Sons are born with the eternal, abundant life of the Father who is dwelling within them. As it is written, *"Whoever shall confess that Jesus is the Son of God, **God abides in him**..."* (1John 4:15). Therefore Sons are God's Life manifested in the flesh. In this affirmation, Sons thank the Father for making them the Way, Truth and Life to those who are lost, deceived and dead from missing the mark. They thank the Father that by their testimony, those who are lost will see the Way, those who are deceived will learn the Truth and those who are dead will be raised to newness of Life in their Christ identity.

7. *"I am the true vine..."* (John 15:1, 5). Jesus was the new Adam, the True Vine connected to Divinity. We were like branches grafted in to that vine, and all its substance flows through us until we and the vine become one vine. The true image and likeness of the invisible God is manifested in and through us, thus making us also the True Vine. Through the vine comes the fruit of the Spirit, *"love, joy, peace, patience, kindness, goodness, faithfulness, gentleness [and] self-control."* (Gal 5:22-23). In this affirmation, Sons thank the Father for making them the true vine that they may bear His Fruit of the Spirit to those whom they come in contact with.

These seven *"I Am"* affirmations are our confession of the Christ identity that we are commanded to put on. These qualities are not of our former Adamic lineage, but of our new Christ lineage, which we simply have inherited by virtue of being sons of the One True Living God. As Paul put it, *"...by the loving-kindness of God, **I Am what I Am**..."* (1Cor 15:10). Not by virtue of anything I have done, but **I Am what I Am** because of what my Heavenly Father has done!

CHAPTER 19
In Spirit and In Truth

In this chapter, we will look at how to access the spirit realm that we may integrate with our true identity. The way of the Tree of Life is all about the spirit realm. The realm of the spirit is the origin of what we see manifested in the natural realm. Therefore the realm of the spirit is the true reality. The inner person is where the spirit of God operates. Once the inner person is renewed, then that renewal manifests in the outer. Jesus talked about the advent of this 'new' way. He told the Samaritan woman, *"the hour is coming, and is now here, when the true worshipers will worship the Father in spirit and truth, for the Father is seeking such people to worship him. God is spirit, and those who worship him must worship **in spirit** and truth..."* (John 4:21-24)

Humanity had been under the paradigm of the Tree of the Knowledge of Good and Evil for four thousand years. Four thousand years of external religion, and of the Father's face being veiled. God had been confined by humanity's distorted opinion as dwelling at Jerusalem in the Temple there. However, the truth was that God is spirit, not restricted in time nor location. He is omnipresent. Yet religions restrict God to particular buildings, referring to them as the *'house of God.'* The truth that Jesus brought was that humanity was the *'house'* that God really dwelt in. The apostle of Christ wrote, *"Do you not know that **you are God's temple** and that God's Spirit dwells in you?"* (1Cor 3:16). God is to be worshipped from within, not in external man-made structures. Church buildings are not *'Houses of God,'* they are places for fellowship. The dwelling of God is not in the building, it is within the Sons of God.

Jesus announced to this nameless woman, two thousand years ago, that the Father was at that time restoring to humanity the way of the Tree of Life, the way of the spirit and truth. Humanity must worship *'in spirit,'* because it is *'in the spirit realm'* that God's true character is experienced and encountered. It is in the spirit realm that the Truth about God's opinion resides. Humanity must enter the spirit realm, for it is in the spirit realm that the Father dwells. Further, the spirit realm was within humanity, for God dwells within. Jesus enlightened the people of his time by letting them know, *"the kingdom of God is not coming in ways that can be observed, nor will they say, 'Look, here it is!' or 'There!' for behold, **the kingdom of God is within you."*** (Luke 17:20-21)

» *Humanity must worship 'in spirit,' because it is 'in the spirit realm' that God's true character is experienced and encountered. It is in the spirit realm that the Truth about God's opinion resides. Humanity must enter the spirit realm, for it is in the spirit realm that the Father dwells.*

In Christ, I am called to realize the awesome reality of my true identity. My acceptance of what my Father has provided for me, is likened to me putting on a royal garment. In the ancient times, and to a certain extent even now, when one becomes a king, the royal robe and a crown bestow a certain glory to that person. We never see the ancient kings portrayed in common clothing. They are always wonderfully attired in garments of splendor befitting their office. Likewise, concerning my True Identity, the apostle Paul counseled, *"**put off from you**, as regards your former behavior, **the old humanity which is corrupted** in accord with its seductive desires,"* (Eph 4:22) and *"...**put on the new humanity, having been newly created** according to God in righteousness and holiness of truth..."* (Eph 4:24). The reception of the new birth identity involves a dual action in the spirit, the *'putting off'* of the old Adamic identity, and the *'putting on'* of the *'new humanity,'* which was newly created fully righteous and holy according to the true opinion of God.

In another place he wrote, *"put on the Lord Jesus Christ..."* (Rom 13:14). Here we can see that *the Lord Jesus Christ is the identity that we are called to put on*. Remember, Jesus' humanity was the vessel for his true identity as the *'Son of God.'* So too should our visible humanity be the vessel for our true identity of Sons of God. This is an identity newly created in the image and likeness of God. This *'putting on'* is not a call for us to *'try to be'* Christ. It is not a call to *'imitate'* him. It is an action to be done in the invisible spirit realm where God dwells within us. This action is essentially depicting our reception of God's true opinion of us.

When we think of the action of putting on, we can see that whatever we put on becomes the container in which we are the contents. In simple terms; when *we put on* that container, *we are in* that container. When we *'put on Christ'*, we are placed *'in Christ,'* and we are also hidden in him. The apostle of Christ wrote, *"your life has been hidden with Christ in God..."* (Col 3:3). Thus when we *'put on Christ,'* we put on the realization that God actually sees us as He sees Christ. It is not that God had a different opinion of us, and then suddenly He changes His opinion when we *'put on Christ.'* No, what actually happens, is that *we receive God's actual opinion of us*, when we *'put on Christ!'*

In the natural realm, the garments we put on have no power except what humanity gives to them. Generally speaking, the garments we wear are chosen by us to convey to others who we think we are, or what role we are portraying. Police officers wear police uniforms, nurses wear nurses' outfits etc. However, the police officers must first be trained and qualified as such, before they are allowed to wear the uniform. Thus the uniform does not make the officer, it only identifies the officer.

Similarly, the garment of Christ identifies who we really are in God's opinion! In the past I had put on many identity containers, but none of them were the truth. God has now offered me a new glorious container that is my true identity. When I put on that container, He proceeds to fill it up with Himself. Paul went further, revealing that *"we all, shown as in a mirror the glory of the Lord, with the face uncovered, are transformed into the same image from glory to glory, as from the Spirit of the Lord."* (2Cor 3:18). Powerful! Just as in the natural, we check out our faces in the mirror which shows us our natural identity, so in the spirit, we are also to look in the spiritual mirror to see our true identity. *In that mirror, we see God's unveiled face instead of our own!* What a powerful opinion from God to inform and form my self-awareness and self-perception! Paul was in symbolic terms letting me know that I have the privilege of putting on the Truth of who I really am – God's Beloved Son! In the spirit, *I resemble my Father*, He has begotten me by His Spirit!

In the Spirit Realm

Many Christians have no idea how to operate in the spirit. Let us first begin by considering the metaphor of *'getting dressed'* – *'putting off'* the old and *'putting on'* the new garment. Where do we normally get dressed? Is it out in the public, or is it in a private place? Is it in the street or in our bedroom? If you are like most people, you get dressed in a secret place. We need to understand that the *'putting off'* of the old and the *'putting on'* of the new, needs to happen in the secret place of the mind – in the invisible internal spirit realm. The new identity is a spirit identity, therefore the *'putting off'* of the old identity and *'putting on'* of the new true identity occurs, not symbolically, but in the reality of the spirit realm. For this to be done, the believer must know how to access this realm. It is through the teaching of Jesus' apostles that we gain the bulk of understanding concerning the spirit realm. The apostle Paul especially, wrote about, *"...serving God in spirit..."* (Phil 3:3); *"...live in spirit, ...walk in spirit..."* (Gal 5:25); *"...praying all times in spirit..."* (Eph 6:18).

The spirit realm is the invisible world accessed within the mind. It is in the mind that creation began. At the original creation, God spoke forth what he had already imagined in His mind. According to the narrative, ***"By the word of the LORD the heavens were made***, *and by the breath of his mouth all their multitudes. For he spoke, and it came to be; he commanded, and it stood firm..."* (Ps 33:6,9). We must consider that before a word is spoken, an idea must have been formed. We speak that which had already been formed in our mind. Jesus showed us that *"those things which proceed out of the mouth **come forth from the heart**..."* (Matt 15:18). The heart, or the mind, is the invisible realm of the creative process. Whatever we conceive in the secret bedchamber of our mind, whether good or evil, will eventually manifest in the visible natural world, it will *'come to be'* and *'stand fast.'* Let's see how Jesus taught this principle, *"whatever you ask in prayer, **believe that you have received it**, and it will be yours..."* (Mark 11:24). Notice Jesus instructed that the correct way to pray is *to believe that you have already received the thing you desire.* Where is this belief first conceived? In the internal mind – in the imagination. The mind via the imagination accesses the invisible realm of the spirit. It is in the realm of the spirit that creation begins. The thing that is desired must be conceived in the mind via the imagination. We are instructed to believe (imagine with the intensity of all emotions) that we already have that which we desire. When we have truly imagined the thing desired, we have essentially created it in the spirit. Jesus assures us that if this is done, *then the thing desired will be ours*. In other words, it will manifest in the natural. What Jesus was hinting at was the ability of Sons of God to create in the spirit realm, whatever they desire to receive in the natural. This is how God created, and this is also how His Sons create. First, creation occurs in the mind with the imagination, then that which is created in the invisible, would manifest visibly through the natural agencies and processes.

The new identity that we desire must be put on in the spirit, in order for it to manifest in the natural. We are to believe (imagine with the intensity of all emotions) that we already have that identity which we desire. When this is done, *then the new identity that we have desired will be ours*. In the next chapter, I will reveal how I personally go about *'putting off'* the old identity and *'putting on'* the new true identity – getting dressed in the spirit realm.

CHAPTER 20
How to Access the Spirit Realm

Of all the chapters in this book, this one may be the most valuable. Here I will share with you how I personally go about accessing the realm of the spirit. I am not insisting that the reader adopt these methods. However, these are some of the ways that I have found to be in harmony with all the principles and truths that I have shared in this book. I have personally found these methods to be very fulfilling and rewarding.

Preparing your Prayer Room

If you can afford it, I recommend you reserve a special *'prayer room'* in your home. It should be essentially sound proof. There should be absolutely no disturbances. No phones ringing, no social media beeps or pings, no children calling, no cars honking... You need what Jesus recommended, *"...when you pray, **enter into your inner room**, and having **shut your door**, pray to your Father, the One in secret..."* (Matt 6:6).

If possible, the walls and ceiling should be painted bright white, with no pictures or adornments, or at least a minimum. It should have a comfortable reclining chair. If you don't have a reclining chair, any comfortable chair should do. You should avoid lying down if possible, for this invites a state of drowsiness and sleep. If the window looks out to the sea, the sky or a beautiful landscape of nature, then the window should not be covered. It should be left open if there is no distracting noise outside and if the weather permits. However, if the window is looking out upon buildings or the street, then cover the window with a white curtain. The room should also be brightly lit and cooled with a fan or air-conditioning in the summer, and pleasantly heated in the winter.

» *Jesus' prayer room was upon a mountain at night. It is recorded that "he went out to the mountain to pray, and all night he continued in prayer to God." (Luke 6:12).*

Alternatively, other *'prayer rooms'* could be an isolated spot in nature – a beach, a field, a mountain, a riverside, a park or garden. Even some homes have a flat roof with access thereto. Jesus' prayer room was upon a mountain at night. It is recorded that *"he went out to the mountain to pray, and all night he continued in prayer to God."* (Luke 6:12). The essential thing for an ideal prayer room is absence of distraction, and to be as far removed from the hustle and bustle of everyday life as is possible.

If none of these are achievable, then you may need to create a prayer time at home sometime from midnight to 3 AM, when all are asleep. If possible, turn on the light in whatever room you are in.

Experiencing Oneness with God

I use this method whenever I need a spiritual boost, and generally when I have the time. For this method you need at least 30 minutes of free, completely undisturbed time.

In your prayer room, relax in your reclining chair. Close your eyes and take some time to slow your breathing and calm yourself down. Maybe you could listen to some relaxing music, or you could sing your favorite hymn.

With your eyes closed, imagine yourself floating above a vast ocean of bright yet soft white light that extends in every direction into eternity. The ocean is moving peacefully, but ever so slightly. This ocean, you know to yourself, is God. Spend some time admiring the beauty of this ocean. Imagine at first being afraid of this ocean of light. Then, purposefully, in your mind, allow yourself to gently fall backwards into the ocean of light. As you fall into it, imagine the experience of this soft white light welcoming you into its liquid arms. It's as if it is saying, *'I love you my Son.'* In the ocean you feel the warmth of pure unconditional accepting Love. Say, *"I love you, Father (Daddy, Dad, Da – whatever term of endearment you wish to use). Thank you for loving me unconditionally."* Imagine yourself rejoicing in the Love of your Father. While in the ocean, take a deep breath, inhaling the soft white light of the ocean. As you do this, feel the warm of the light filling your body, beginning at your nostrils, then to your had and gradually down to the extremes of your limbs. You dissolve wonderfully into the ocean, and become one with it. Rejoice in your oneness with your Father. Confess your oneness. Say, *"I am one with my Father, as He is, so am I. I am His Love, I am His Light, I am His Life."* You may use these attributes of God or any other that you deem appropriate according to what has been revealed about God's true character.

Imagine yourself spreading with the ocean throughout the earth. Imagine spreading the love of God throughout the earth. Bless the earth and its inhabitants with your Father's love. Like your Father, you are spirit, formless, endless and full of love. Experience yourself expanding throughout the galaxies.

Remain in this ocean experience as long as you need to, or as long as time allows. Before leaving this spirit realm, declare, *"As it is in the spirit, so is it in the natural."* Then open your eyes.

Putting On Christ in the Spirit

I use this method to integrate fully into the various aspects of my new true identity. For this method you need at least 30 minutes of free, completely undisturbed time, for each aspect that you are integrating.

In your prayer room, relax in your reclining chair. Close your eyes and take some time to slow your breathing and calm yourself down. Maybe you could listen to some relaxing music, or you could sing your favorite hymn.

With your eyes closed, imagine yourself in a bright room with walls, floor and ceiling all glowing pure white. In the middle of the room is a full-length mirror. Walk up to the full-length mirror and look at yourself in it. Take some time to really study your reflection. Now, turn around with your back to the mirror. You now notice a most magnificent looking robe hanging on the wall, directly in front of you. Walk up to the robe and observe it closely. Instead of fabric, it appears to be made entirely of pure soft white light. It glows extremely brightly, so brightly that you have to squint to prevent your eyes from hurting. There are neither visible stitches, seams nor buttons on this garment. Decide you want to put on this robe. First, undress yourself. Then, reach out, take the robe of light and put it on. It is weightless and feels soft as a puff of breeze. The robe reaches exactly to your feet, and fits you perfectly. As you put it on, the light from the robe seems to cause your skin to glow bright white as well. Your whole body begins to glow and you feel warm and confident. Whatever fears and insecurities you may have had are suddenly gone. You can feel your face glowing dazzling bright white, almost as the sun. Turn completely around and look at yourself in the mirror. You look almost like a bright star.

Take some time to check out yourself in the mirror. Say, *"Thank you Father (Daddy, Dad, Da – whatever term of endearment you wish to use) for transforming me into your likeness and glory. I love you."*

At this point, you can pick any of the Christ confessions listed in Chapter 13 or any of the Seven Christ affirmations listed in Chapter 18 and confess them, giving thanks to your heavenly Father, while looking in the mirror.

For example, here's how to confess the second of the Seven Affirmations of Christ.

While looking at your glowing self in the mirror, you hear a soft whispering voice saying in your ear, *"I have made you a light to the world."* Take some time to appreciate what this means. Rejoice in this aspect of your new identity. Say, *"Thank you Father (Daddy, Dad, Da – whatever term of endearment you wish to use), for making me a Light of the World. I love you."* Picture yourself, where ever you go, as a bright glowing light like the sun. Picture people who are discouraged and depressed becoming hopeful and happy to be in your presence. Picture folks thanking you for being a blessing to their lives.

Say, *"Thank you Father, I am a blessing to everyone with whom I encounter."*

Before leaving this spirit realm, declare, *"As it is in the spirit, so is it in the natural."* Then open your eyes.

In subsequent sessions when you enter this room, you can choose to be already dressed in the robe of light. Thus you can go straight to the mirror and begin confessing.

Praying in the Spirit

The apostle of Christ counseled that Sons ought to be *"praying in the Spirit in every season..."* (Eph 6:18). The word 'prayer' or to 'pray' comes from the Greek words 'euchomai' which means *'wish'* and *'pros'* which means *'towards.'* It literally means to *'wish for.'* Thus prayer is the communication of our wishes to our Father, who is able to make those wishes come true.

Some prayers are our wishes concerning ourselves and situations affecting us, some prayers are our wishes concerning others and situations affecting them. There are prayers where we are seeking answers to life's puzzles, as well as guidance in making decisions. There are prayers which are requested by friends, loved ones and brethren.

It is recommended that we always be communicating our wishes to our Father in our minds, wherever we may be. However, there are times when, for the sake of needing to really focus on exactly what it is we need to ask for, it is necessary to have a *'sit down'* with our Father and have a *'face to face'* conversation with Him. These are the times when we can use the *'Oneness with God'* method to help bring us into the presence of God.

When it comes to prayer, God desires to unite with us from within to assist us in getting our prayers on target. We are told, *"the Spirit helps us in our weakness. For we do not know what to pray for as we ought, but the Spirit itself expresses our request for us with groanings too deep for words."* (Rom 8:26). The Spirit communicates our emotions directly to our Father. When a situation is troubling us, the emotions we feel such as fear, heaviness of heart or discouragement, all need to be communicated to the Father, because the real issue we want resolved is not the external situation, but the negative effects that we are experiencing within. What we really wish for is a situation where we or the person we are praying for, are at peace, secure, happy, confident, loved etc. These are all positive emotions or 'spirits.' So when we come to our Father, it is essentially for Him to work out the situation, so that the negative 'spirits' are removed and replaced by the positive 'spirits.' This is the essence of praying in the spirit. It is assessing what is the spirit of any given situation. If that situation's 'spirit' is negative or ungodly, then our request or wish should be for that situation to be transformed into a positive or Godly 'spirit.'

I do not intend this book to be a prayer manual, so I will just outline a few principles that should help you in the way.

Principles of Praying in the Spirit

- Determine if your request is in harmony with the New Creation. Is it a request for life, love, abundance, peace, faith, health, security, joy, patience, self-control, etc? It is essential that you are asking according to your Father's will. He will not grant a request that is not in harmony with His own character.

- Begin your prayer session by entering the presence of God by using the *'Oneness with God'* method.

- Try to present only one request per session, usually the most pressing one. Ideally any new session should be attempted after 24-hours or more later.

- While in the presence of God, bring to mind the situation for which you are requesting the Lord's intervention.

- Allow the negative emotions that you experience as a result of the present situation to well-up in you. This prepares you to express your request not in human words, but in the language of the spirit, the emotion that the situation generates in you. Some examples of emotions that are felt in these situations are powerlessness, fear, pain, indignation over injustice, lack of worth, indebtedness, bondage, hopelessness, depression, discouragement, emptiness, lacking direction, confusion, etc.

- Communicate to your Father how the situation makes you feel by sharing just the emotions, *not your words, only your emotions* with Him. This is where you will experience the *'groanings of the spirit.'*

- Now in your mind, imagine the situation as if it is a big movie poster. Put forth your hands, grab that poster, fold it up, fold over fold, until it is a tiny as you can get it. Then toss it away, as far as you can throw it.

- Now, imagine the situation completely transformed. Imagine that God has answered the prayer even beyond your expectation. When you view the transformed situation in your mind's eye, think about how the transformation makes you feel. Allow these *positive emotions* to fill you to the fullest. Your Father will not answer a request that brings about negative emotions. Examples of positive emotions are peace, love, joy, confidence, victory, etc. Examples of negative emotions are hate, spite, arrogance, selfishness etc.

- Share with your Father how the transformed situation is now making you feel. Again, share the emotions, *not your words*, with Him.

- Now, allow yourself to bask in the peaceful assurance that your Father will answer your wish perfectly, with either the exact thing requested, its perfect equivalent, or something even better.

- Thank your Father, and let Him know that you love Him.

- End the session as recommended in the *'Oneness Method.'*

- During the days, weeks or months after, as you go about your daily life, continue to thank God for intervening in the situation.

Conclusion

If you apply these concepts, and even modify them to suit your individual style and circumstances, your devotions and prayer life would never be boring or monotonous. Not only that, you would begin to see amazing things happening in your life. The powerful word of God has begun working within and without to bring about God's will. As you have put on Christ in the invisible realm of the spirit, he will manifest through you in the visible realm of the natural. This is what Jesus was referring to when he said, *"Your will be done as in heaven, so also upon earth."* (Matt 6:10). When God's will is accomplished in the spirit realm, it is sure to manifest in the natural realm.

Any time faith is exercised in the Opinion of God, its power is immediately activated. As we confess our identity in harmony with God's Opinion, the promise from the Father is, *"so shall My Word be that goes out from My mouth; it shall not return to Me empty, but **it shall accomplish that which I purpose**, and shall succeed in the thing for which I sent it."* (Isa 55:11). Rest assured, our Father's word concerning us, will succeed in accomplishing His purpose. It cannot fail! This is how Sons of God keep His New Creation Sabbath, by resting with God in a confident trust in His Character, Power and Promise. Shalom!

I wholeheartedly hope that this book has been a blessing to you. I know that most likely you may need to re-read this book several times. There is a lot in it that might be missed the first time reading it.

I hope that this book has served to bring you to the knowledge of the insanely good news of our Loving Father and His Opinion of us. What's next? That's for you and the Lord to determine. We are encouraged to *"grow in [God's] loving-kindness and in knowledge of our Lord and Savior Jesus Christ. To him be the glory both now and to the day of eternity. Amen!"* (2Pet 3:18)

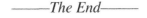

The End

I hope this book has been a blessing to you!

If you are looking for a resource on how to live in your new identity, consider subscribing to

The New Kosmos Masterclass

This online seminar Presents with your Identity in Christ, Positions you in the Kingdom of God, and Prepares you to Live Abundantly.

Receive clarity on what is available to you as a Kingdom Citizen, and a more detailed picture of your potential as a Child of God.

The New Kosmos Masterclass

Many have come to discover their true identity through the 'Living in the New Kosmos' Masterclass.

Obtain the clearest understanding of your Identity in Christ.

Live successfully and victoriously a life of Peace, Purpose and Prosperity.

Sign Up Now!

Scan the QR Code or go to *newkosmos.us/masterclass*

Made in United States
Orlando, FL
13 July 2024

48925974R00085